Dr. LAWRENCE A. NIXON
and the
WHITE PRIMARY

Dr. Lawrence A. Nixon

Dr. LAWRENCE A. NIXON and the WHITE PRIMARY

by CONREY BRYSON

Texas Western Press

THE UNIVERSITY OF TEXAS AT EL PASO
SOUTHWESTERN STUDIES No. 42

INTRODUCTION TO SECOND EDITION

An introduction to the second edition of this work cannot be written but in a spirit of rejoicing. Recall that, when Dr. Nixon filed his first suit against those who had denied him the right to vote, his children could attend but one school in El Paso. He could live only in certain areas of the city. He would be denied service at most first class hotels, motels and restaurants. Although fully qualified medically, he could not be a member of the local medical society and could practice at most local hospitals only if sponsored by a white doctor. As chronicled in the text, these barriers have all been removed. Dr. Nixon's daughter, Edna Nixon McIver, wife of an Albuquerque physician, has chronicled a list of pertinent events facilitated by the extended right to vote, since her father's challenge to voting restrictions in El Paso:

August 29, 1957 - Congress passed the first federal civil rights legislation since 1875.

May 6, 1960 - President Eisenhower signed the Civil Rights Act of 1960.

July 2, 1964 - President Lyndon B. Johnson signed a civil rights bill with public accommodations and employment sections.

February 21, 1965 - President Lyndon B. Johnson signed an extensive voting rights bill.

November 7, 1967 - Carl B. Stokes was elected mayor of Cleveland, Ohio, the first black to become mayor of a major American city. Richard G. Hatcher was elected mayor of Gary, Indiana.

November 17, 1972 - Sixteen black candidates were elected to the Congress of the United States. Andrew Young, of Atlanta, was the first black elected to Congress from the deep South since the reconstruction era. Also elected for the first time were Barbara Jordan of Texas and Yvonne Braithwaite Burke of California.

October 27, 1981 - Andrew Young, former U.N. Ambassador, elected mayor of Atlanta, Georgia.

November 8, 1983 - W. Wilson Goode became the first black mayor of Philadelphia.

February 10, 1989 - Ronald Brown was elected chairman of the Democratic National Committee—the same party which denied Dr. Nixon the vote in 1924.

November 2, 1989 - David Dinkins became the first black mayor of New York City.

March 16, 1991 - Rev. Emanuel Cleaver became the first black mayor of Kansas City, Missouri.

June 18, 1991 - Wellington Webb elected mayor of Denver, Colorado.

Dr. Nixon's widow, Drusilla, lived to see most of the progress. She died May 10, 1991, at the home of her daughter, Edna, in Albuquerque. She did not live to see a climaxing event in El Paso, on November 13, 1991, when a new elementary school, at 11141 Loma Roja in far northeast El Paso, was dedicated as the Dr. Lawrence A. Nixon School.

The dedicatory program was highlighted with the reading, by a fourth grade student, of a poem about Dr. Nixon. Its last verse carries the spirit of the dedication:

Dr. Nixon, all of us are special because of you.
We meet in this school, vibrant, alive, and brand new,
Named after a quiet, dedicated, and successful man,
A Pioneer in this City, a Pioneer in this land.

It was fitting that an elementary school should be named for Dr. Nixon, for his family is firmly dedicated to the highest purposes of education and life. At the close of her remarks at the dedication, Edna read tributes to their grandfather from four of her children who could not be present. The educational achievements of the children of Dr. and Mrs. W. J. McIver are impressive:

Daughter Beth graduated from Hunter College, New York City, in December 1991, with a degree in film production, photography and education.

Daughter Angela is working on her master's degree in education at Temple University.

Daughter Stephanie is working on her PhD. in Clinical Psychology at Ohio State University.

Son Ben finished Morehouse College in Atlanta in May 1992, with a degree in economics and business.

Son Bill is working on his PhD. in computer science at the University of Colorado.

The eldest and adopted son, Mike (survivor of the tragic accident that claimed Edna's sister Dorothy and her family), lives in El Paso, is married and has two sons, and owns an air-conditioning and plumbing business. He and his family were present at the dedication of the Dr. Lawrence A. Nixon School.

A quotation from the joint tribute by Angela McIver Clarke and Stephanie McIver might well climax this new introduction:

"Naming a school after our grandfather is certainly an honor. However, it is also an obligation to view all children, regardless of race, class, or ethnic origin as potential contributors to the progress of our country. His legacy has lived on in our hearts and has inspired us to achieve."

SATURDAY, JULY 26, 1924, was cloudy and hot in El Paso. It was one of those days when the clouds could give relief only if they would produce some welcome moisture. Standing in line in the heat, in front of the polling place at the East El Paso Fire Station, 2317 Texas Street, a tall, slender El Paso physician, Dr. Lawrence A. Nixon, felt especially conspicuous. He was a negro,* and this was a Democratic primary.

He hoped that the poll tax receipt he carried in his pocket was correct and in order. He checked it again as he approached the voting judges and clerks. It was poll tax receipt No. 3486, issued January 15, 1924, to L. A. Nixon, 2029 Myrtle Avenue, El Paso, Texas, in voting precinct No. 9. It showed he was forty-one, a resident of Texas for forty-one years, and of the City and County of El Paso for fourteen years. Under sex and race he was listed as "male, black." The receipt said "received the sum of one and 75/100 dollars in payment of poll tax for the year 1923. The said taxpayer being duly sworn by me says that the above is correct, all of which I certify. R. D. Richey, Tax Collector, El Paso County, Texas, by P. A. Candelaria, Deputy." An endorsement on the back read "Voted May 7, 1924."[1]

Dr. Nixon may have smiled when he recalled that vote. On April 17, he had headed a committee of negroes who appeared before Mayor R. M. Dudley and the El Paso City Council to request

---

* Most dictionaries and style books capitalize the word Negro. In this treatise, the laws on which Dr. Nixon's suits were based used a small "n." The lower case "n" was also used in the Supreme Court decision in *Nixon v. Herndon* and in the preliminary portion of the *Nixon v. Condon* decision. Because of these facts and the frequent use of the word in this treatise, the lower case will be used except in direct quotations using the capital "N."

a swimming pool for negroes at Washington Park. The Council was considering building a pool for the negroes at Douglass School, the only school in El Paso negro children were permitted to attend. Dr. Nixon's committee protested a lack of transportation facilities to Douglass, and said the Washington Park site would be much more convenient for most negro families. Mayor Dudley decided on a firm stand. He had been elected a year earlier in a showdown battle with the Ku Klux Klan, which was still active, and he did not want to do anything that might cause trouble between the races. A negro pool at Washington Park might do just that. "There has always existed in El Paso the best possible feeling between negroes and whites, and I do not think it would be the better part of wisdom to disturb that feeling," the mayor said. Then he suggested the negro community support the bond issue on May 7—there would be enough money there to build a swimming pool for them.[2]

On May 7th, Dr. Nixon had voted, but he knew he would not be permitted to vote again this July 26. The fact that negroes would be turned away from the polls had not been widely publicized. In the three El Paso newspapers, there had been only one such notice. It had appeared on page 20 of the *El Paso Times*, July 20, 1924, under a headline "George Pendell Withdraws his Fight on Vowell." Far down in the article was a list of rules that were being distributed to all election judges for the Democratic Primary. Of the twenty-seven rules, the shortest was number twenty-six: "Negroes cannot vote in the Primary."

Despite such meager publicity, the word had gotten around. In order to survive, minorities often develop a highly efficient grapevine. This was especially true in El Paso. More western than southern, El Paso reflected variations in the pattern of extreme segregation. The word got around: this restaurant will serve you, this one will not. This small southside hotel will accept negro guests. Negroes are being permitted to buy homes in this southeast El Paso subdivision. At this particular performance at Liberty Hall, negroes will be seated in the balcony, whites on the main floor. Dr. Nixon and other negroes had previously voted in Democratic primaries, but the word had gotten around, and he was the only black man in line when he presented his poll tax to the election judges. He knew he would not be permitted to vote. What he did not know was that twenty years would pass before he could walk into that polling place, present his poll tax receipt, and vote.

Early Negro Leaders

In the years following the Civil War, Texas negroes had taken seriously the fourteenth and fifteenth amendments to the national constitution. Under the leadership of men of considerable ability in their own race, they accepted the constitutional guarantee that they should not be deprived of their equal rights by any state and the specific guarantee that they should not be deprived of their right to vote because of "race, color, or previous condition of servitude."

In the earliest years of the postwar period, Texas negroes were nearly all Republicans, for the Democratic party was considered the party of the Confederacy; however, the popularized picture of ignorant blacks in state leggislatures, blindly doing the will fo their Republican masters, simply was not a true picture of the Lone Star State. The black race produced men of outstanding ability and some of them were dominating figures in Republican politics of the state and nation.[3]

An interesting example is Norris Wright Cuney, who is described by Governor James Stephen Hogg's biographer as ranking "among the greatest political leaders of Texas."[4] Cuney was the son of a white planter who came to Texas from Louisiana in 1842, and settled on Sunnyside Plantation near Hempstead, Texas. Colonel Philip Cuney fathered eight children by his slave, Adeline Stuart. Norris Wright Cuney was the fourth of these, and by no means the only example of children of dissolute white parents who rose in the ranks of their political opposition.[5] He was a power in Texas politics from 1872 to 1896, and served as Texas Republican national committeeman from 1885 to 1896. His enemies considered him ruthless, but his friends found him a tower of strength, at a time when Texas influence in the councils of government in Washington was highly prized.[6] Negro political leaders were not only prominent in the Republican party; they were influential in the various political reforms of the 1890s. Many of them deserted the Republicans to help elect the reform Democrat, James Stephen Hogg, in 1892. Others were influential in the birth of the Texas

Populist party, which became a major influence in the Populist revolt, a movement which brought reforms to both existing parties. In Texas, the outstanding negro Populist was J. B. Rayner, who deserted the Republican party in the early nineties. Rayner was born a slave, the natural son of a white father, Kenneth Rayner, then prominent in the public life of North Carolina. The son became not only a respected political leader, but a distinguished educator, the president of Conroe Normal and Industrial College of Conroe, Texas.[7]

Lawrence D. Rice has chronicled the work of nearly three score Texas negroes who served as either Texas legislators or delegates to Texas Constitutional Conventions between 1868 and 1898. They were influential in drafting both the Constitution of 1869 and the present one, adopted in 1876. Politicians of both paties spoke with respect of such men as Meshach Roberts, the giant blacksmith from Marshall, and W. M. Burton whose outstanding service as a Texas state senator won him a gift of a gold-headed ebony cane. But the brilliant record ends dismally. The last two negroes to serve in the Texas legislature were N. H. Haller and R. L. Smith, who served in the late nineties.[8] Not until 1966 was a negro again elected to either house of the Texas legislature.

Decline of Negro Political Voice

The transition of a society from a condition where the negro had political power and influence to the picture of a lone black physician standing in line at the polling place, and knowing he would not be permitted to vote, is not easy to trace. In the later phases of the transition, in the early 1920s, the lately resurrected Ku Klux Klan had a part, but the negro had already been quite effectively disfranchised much earlier. By the turn of the century, his political power in Texas had become negligible.[9] It began to fail when he tried to make his political voice effective in other quarters than the Republican party.

With the rise of the Populist movement, the Republican party found itself widely characterized as the party of big business, and it is not surprising that politically conscious negroes began to find common cause with Populists, the People's Party, the Greenback Party, and even the Democratic. As indicated earlier, many negroes helped in the election of the reform-minded Texas governor, James S. Hogg. Not only did negroes desert the Republicans, but in large measure the Republican Party deserted the black man. A movement toward what was called "lily-white Republicanism" discouraged negro participation in the party councils, and brought a serious split in party ranks.[10]

Efforts to Enter Democratic Party

When blacks tried to enter the Democratic party ranks, they found their way effectively blocked. There seems to have been no central direction of this activity, but examples from several counties in the black belt will show how it was accomplished. In Huntsville, Texas, the last negro elected to public office was a constable named Joshua Green. To discourage him from taking office, the county judge raised the bond requirement to $20,000. When he raised the satisfactory sureties for that amount, various residents of the county simply "intervened" and "persuaded" him not to serve.[11]

In Athens, Texas, as early as 1883, negroes were elected mayor, city attorney, and city marshal. White aldermen simply refused to serve with them. Because of this opposition, the legally elected negroes never came forward to assume their duties, and the white incumbents continued to hold office. Even when the incumbent mayor died, the elected negro refused to assume his place, because of the widespread objections.[12]

In Marshall, Texas, the community where Dr. L. A. Nixon was born, agreement to exclude negroes from political life came early. Although the population of the county in 1876 was 68 percent negro, the candidates in the Democratic Primary agreed that "no colored voters be allowed to vote in the Primary Election unless the judges have positive information that the applicant has heretofore voted the Democratic ticket."[13] When Republicans won the election, white political leaders of Harrison County began to look to other methods of achieving white supremacy. In 1878, they formed a "Citizens Party," officially described as nonpartisan, but it was understood that the purpose was to insure the election of white candidates. The election of 1880 ended with sixty-five persons being charged in Federal court with intimidation and the use of fraud and violence against negroes to keep them from exercising their right of suffrage. Nearly three thousand witnesses were heard. Forty-five of the defendants pleaded guilty and were assessed fines of one dollar each, plus court costs. By 1881, the Citizens Party controlled local politics in Harrison County, and negroes were completely excluded from local elections.[14]

Violence erupted on both sides in the widespread efforts to disfranchise negroes in the Texas "black belt." In 1886, negroes were accused of killing the son of a Democratic candidate in Washington County because they thought he intended to steal a ballot box. A white mob took three negro leaders from jail and lynched them. This, and similar episodes in Matagorda, Wharton, and Fort Bend counties led to a United States Senate investigation, which only served to prove widespread guilt on the part of both sides in the conflict, and did little to prevent the onrushing disfran- chisement of the Texas negro.[15] That he was really disfranchised and not merely confined to the Republican party is evident from the fact that the Republican vote in Washington County decreased by 40 percent from 1884 to 1892.[16]

The Texas Jaybird Case

One important phase of negro disfranchisement was to be aired before the nation in a celebrated Supreme Court case known as the Texas Jaybird Case, which was not decided until 1953.[17] A young man's Democratic club formed in Fort Bend County, Texas, in 1888, came to be known as the "Jaybird Club," while its oppo- nents, who favored co-operation with negroes of the county, were designated as "Woodpeckers." The rivalry between these two white factions grew into violence over the question of negro involvement in politics, and resulted in the killing of at least one member of each faction, and in a pitched battle in the streets of Richmond, Texas. It also resulted in the complete control of party politics in Fort Bend County by the Jaybirds. On October 3, 1889, the Jaybirds drew up their constitution and bylaws. As summarized in a history of Fort Bend County, every white citizen was eligible for membership. Members pledged themselves to support the nominees of the Jaybirds Association and to serve as sureties on the bonds of any association nominees elected to any office. Any white resident of the county who led a faction in opposition to the association was considered and treated as a social and political outcast. No member could become a candidate for political office without the endorsement of the party's membership.[18]

The Jaybird Club quickly spread to other counties, and when the case finally reached the Supreme Court, Justice Hugo Black, who wrote the decision, reviewed the history of the Jaybirds Association back to 1899: "The Jaybird primary has become an integral part, indeed the only effective part, of the electoral process that determines who shall rule and govern in the County. The effect of the whole procedure, Jaybird primary plus Democratic Primary, plus general election, is to do precisely that which the fifteenth amendment forbids—strip negroes of every vestige of influence in selecting the officials who control the county matters that intimately touch the daily lives of citizens."

The Poll Tax Amendment

With such a catalog of restrictions already in effect, it can hardly be claimed that the poll tax amendment to the Texas Constitution, instituted in 1902, was intended primarily to disfranchise the negro. Dean Abner V. McCall, of Baylor University School of Law, gives his explanation of the reason for the 1902 amendment in his "History of Texas Elections Law" published as a preface to the Texas Election Code:

> Contrary to general opinion now, this amendment was not the result of racial prejudice, but, was sponsored by the reform element in the Democratic party and the Prohibitionists as an election law reform. It was the repeated charge of these groups that the "big interests" and the liquor interests controlled thousands of negro and Latin-American voters through paid "influence" men. The poll-tax was designed to decrease this controlled vote. It also provided an automatic system of mandatory registration of voters without use of the hated phrase calculated to stir bitter memories of the reconstruction.[19]

As the present writer stated in a previous article, a good case can be made for the claim that controlled voting in El Paso County was in large measure responsible for the institution of the poll tax in 1902, and El Paso's State Senator W. W. Turney and State Representative W. W. Bridgers gave enthusiastic support to the

amendment.[20] Nevertheless, the poll tax was one more deterrent
to impoverished negroes, who usually believed in January that
$1.75 could be spent in more useful ways than the doubtful assur-
ance of the right to vote many months later.

By 1910, the year Dr. Nixon arrived in El Paso, the negro
was disfranchsied in those Texas counties where it mattered. In El
Paso, it could make little difference whether he voted or not. The
1920 census showed a negro population of only 1,562, or 3.0
percent of the population in El Paso County. The 1920 census
showed a decrease in number to 1,548 and a percentage of 1.5.
In such counties as El Paso, political leaders could afford to be
generous to the blacks, and Dr. Nixon voted regularly in both
general and primary elections.[21]

The Klan Influence

With the negro so completely ineffective in Texas politics, it
is difficult to find a reason for the action taken by the Texas
legislature in May 1923, specifically denying him the right to vote
in Democratic primaries.[22] The historian is tempted to blame the
Ku Klux Klan, even though the specific action of presenting the
bill to the legislature and securing its passage cannot be traced to
Klan sources. There was widespread Klan influence throughout
Texas politics in 1923. In the 1922 election, the Klan candidate
for the United States Senate, Earle B. Mayfield, was selected for
the candidacy through the personal intervention of Hiram Evans,
imperial kligrapp (National Secretary) of the Klan, and preparing
for his advancement to imperial wizard, the top man of the Klan
in all the nation, the following year. In a bitterly fought Democratic
runoff primary, Mayfield defeated the controversial but still effective former governor, James E. Ferguson, by more than 44,000
votes.[23] Charging illegal activities by the Klan, Mayfield's oppo-
nents challenged his election before the United States Senate Committee on Privileges and Elections. The hearings did much to pub-
licize the Ku Klux Klan, and little to curb its activities, and on
February 3, 1925, after he had already been serving for two years,
the Senate voted unanimously to seat Earle B. Mayfield. [24]

Mayfield's victory was but one of many in 1922 and 1923
by the Klan and its sympathizers. The order probably had a major-

ity in the 38th Texas Legislature which met in January 1923. In municipal elections that same year, the hooded order gained control of city governments in Dallas, Fort Worth, and Wichita Falls, although it lost the elections in San Antonio and El Paso.[25] Still, despite such evidences of Klan control, it cannot be shown that there was any widespread campaign, by the Klan or anyone else, to deprive the negro of any opportunities he might still have to vote in Democratic primaries. The bill which denied him such rights came in without fanfare and was passed almost without notice.

The Davenport-Beasley Bill

The bill was in peril from the date it was introduced, April 25, as H. B. 72, in the House of Representatives by D. S. Davenport of Dallas and Clifton E. Beasley, of Sulphur Springs. This bill stated, in part, "In no event shall a negro participate in a Democratic Primary in the State of Texas."[26] Before the day was out, Lieutenant Governor Davidson had ruled that this bill and a number of others were out of order because they were not listed on Governor Pat M. Neff's call for a second special session of the Legislature.[27] The governor took care of that deficiency the following day. Avoiding any mention of negro voting in primaries, he submitted an amended call for the special session, listing the need to amend the primary election laws of Texas.[28] This cleared the way for action on H. B. 72, and also on a similar bill, S. B. 44, introduced in the Senate May 1, by R. S. Bowers, of Caldwell, Texas.[29] The governor's hurried action in removing an almost insurmountable legislative obstacle has not been adequately explained. If pressure by the Ku Klux Klan was involved, it was not evident. The Klan had neither endorsed nor opposed Neff in the 1922 campaign, and he had been elected on a law and order campaign, keeping himself largely above the Klan controversy.[30]

With the governor's vague listing on the agenda for the special session, the bill could move through legislative channels, but its progress was impeded again and again. The Senate bill was referred to the Committee on Privileges and Elections, and on May 3, 1923, Senator John Davis, of Dallas, chairman of the committee, submitted to the floor an adverse report by the Committee, recommending that the bill "do not pass." The Senate *Journal* does not show that there was a minority report. Senator Bowers, the bill's author, nevertheless managed to secure passage of a motion that the bill be printed in the *Journal*. This paved the way for the chair to lay the bill before the Senate on May 8, and Bowers used the parliamentary maneuver of moving that the minority report be adopted, thus reversing the action of the committee. His motion passed by a voice vote. On a roll call vote of 24-0 the bill was moved to final passage, after being declared an emergency due to the crowded calendar. It was then passed by a voice vote.[31] El Paso had no representative in the State Senate when the bill was passed. Senator Richard M. Dudley had resigned to become mayor of El Paso and a successor had not yet been elected.

In the House, the Davenport-Beasley bill was passed without difficulty, on May 8, after being amended to incorporate the language of the Senate bill. Meanwhile, the Senate bill itself moved over to the House on the same day, and on May 9, the House passed S. B. 44 on second reading and Representative Davenport moved that the three-day rule be suspended, and the bill be immediately placed before the House for third reading and final passage. The vote for final passage was 93-10. El Paso Representatives Adrian Pool and J. E. Quaid voted for the bill. Representative R. B. Stevens of El Paso was absent.[32]

Representative R. A. Baldwin, of Slaton, asked the privilege of making an explanation regarding his vote. He told the House, "I seriously doubt the constitutionality of Senate Bill number 44, expressly disfranchising negroes in primary elections, and see in it possibilities for serious legal complications and many contests of primary elections. For these reasons I cannot vote for it." Nevertheless, Baldwin did not vote against the bill; he simply voted "present." It was hard to find a strong advocate for the disfranchised negro in the Texas State Legislature of 1923. On May 10, Speaker R. E. Seagler signed the bill and sent it to the governor.[33]

The bill was presented to Governor Pat M. Neff for his approval on May 10. Under the Texas Constitution, the governor has a ten-day period, while the legislature is in session, in which to cast a veto. After five days had passed, on May 15, the legislature adjourned. The governor then had three alternatives: he could sign the bill, let it become law in ten days without his signature, or cast a veto by sending the bill to the secretary of state with his reasons for the veto. Such vetoes by the governor of Texas are frequent, and are absolute, there being no opportunity for the legislature to override the veto. Governor Neff could have killed the legislation. He could have indicated his approval by signing it. Instead, he simply did nothing, and the bill became law without his signature.[34]

As enacted, Senate Bill 44 read:

Be it enacted by the Legislature of the State of Texas:

Sec. 1: That Article 3093 of the Revised Civil Statutes of the State of Texas, of 1911, be amended by adding thereto a new section to be known as Article 3093a, to read as follows:

Article 3093a: All qualified voters under the laws and constitution of the State of Texas who are bona fide members of the Democratic Party shall be eligible to participate in any Democratic party primary election, provided such voter complies with all laws and rules governing party primary elections; however, in no event shall a negro be eligible to participate in a Democratic primary election held in the State of Texas, and should a negro vote in a Democratic Primary election, such ballot shall be void, and election officials are herein directed to throw out such ballot and not count the same.

Sec. 2: Also amending Article 3089 of the Revised Civil Statutes of the State of Texas, of 1911, by adding thereto a new section to be known as Article 3089a, and to read as follows:

Article 3089a: All supervisors, judges and clerks of any election shall be qualified voters of the election precinct in which they are named to serve.

Sec. 3: The crowded condition of the Legislative calendar creates imperative public necessity making necessary the suspension of the constitutional rule requiring bills to be read on three several days in each House, and this Act shall take effect from and after its passage, and said rule is herby suspended and it is so enacted.[35]

The Challenge to the Bill

There were several good reasons why El Paso should be the place where the first legal challenge would be made against this disfranchisement of the negro. The city had an active chapter of the National Association for the Advancement of Colored People, organized in 1910, the same year as the national organization. Dr. Nixon, who came to El Paso in January that year, had been one of its charter members.[36] It was a good place to find organizational

support for a suit, and a good place to look for the right person
to file the suit.

A letter from Attorney Fred C. Knollenberg, dated July 25,
1924, the day before Dr. Nixon attempted to vote in the Democratic
Primary, reviewed the qualifications of the person in whose name
the suit would be filed. Knollenberg had just been employed by
the NAACP to file the suit. Dr. Nixon had already been selected
by the organization as the man who would attempt to vote, but
Knollenberg again outlined the necessary qualifications in a letter
to L. W. Washington, president of the El Paso Chapter, National
Association for the Advancement of Colored People:

> To test the validity of Chapter 32, Laws of the First Called Session
> 38th Legislature, which provide that the negro shall not be able to vote
> in the Democratic Primary, wish to say that you should proceed as follows:
> 1. Select 1 or more negroes.
> 2. They must be bona fide members of the Democratic Party.
> 3. They must have paid their poll tax or obtained a certificate of
> exemption, and they must be registered in the precinct of their residence.
> 4. See that he has a poll-tax and that it is properly made out, and
> his voting precinct stated or that he is registered on the list of qualified
> voters. Request the presiding judge for ballot in the voter's precinct ten-
> dering him the poll-tax receipt; if the ballot is refused and the right to
> vote is refused, just request the name of the judge or judges refusing
> same, and ask them to please note on something that the person that has
> made application to vote was refused under Article 3093a, of the Statutes
> of the State of Texas.
> I remain yours very truly,
>   Fred C. Knollenberg.[37]

Only in a place such as El Paso, an area where negroes had
a high degree of political consciousness, and yet were not numerous
enough to challenge the white power structure, would the NAACP
be likely to find a negro who paid his poll tax and had participated
enough in party politics that he could be legally described as a
"bona fide member of the Democratic party." In the areas of the
state where blacks were more numerous, the Jaybird Primary and
less formal restrictions and intimidations had long kept the negroes
from participation.

Someone Who is Not Afraid

William Pickens, field secretary of the NAACP, had personally selected Dr. Nixon to be the man who would challenge the state law. Pickens, an eloquent speaker, had come to El Paso and held a rally at Liberty Hall. A band from Douglass High School, then a segregated negro school, provided the music, and Pickens told the all-negro audience that the organization he represented meant to challenge a Texas law which was in violation of both the fourteenth and fifteenth amendments to the Constitution of the United States. After reviewing the El Paso physician's legal qualifications to file the suit, Pickens outlined some further conditions: Could Dr. Nixon give the necessary time for any required legal appearances? Would he and other members of the El Paso NAACP help to finance the court battle, which would probably be long and difficult?

And, finally, said the field secretary: "We are looking for someone who is not afraid."[38]

Dr. Nixon must have had second thoughts about his quick assurance that he was not afraid. He read the newspapers, and the annual reports of the NAACP which regularly chronicled the various lynchings throughout the previous year. Certainly he had read the story of John K. Smitherman, a prominent Tulsa, Oklahoma, negro who had been accused of registering negroes to vote in the Democratic primaries, and of being discourteous to a Tulsa white woman. Smitherman later testified in court that at 2 a.m., March 10, 1922, three masked men forced him from his home, beat him with a pistol butt when he struggled with them, and shoved him into an automobile. He was driven to a hillside near Tulsa, chained to a tree, and confronted by twelve men, eight of them wearing masks. The accusations against him were repeated, some of the men spat in his face, and the masked men lashed him with a blacksnake whip. After the whipping, one of the men cut off the negro's ear with a pocketknife, and tried to make him eat the ear. When this was unsuccessful, the mob began to break up, after warning Smitherman to leave Tulsa and never come back. Instead, he stayed and told his story to the courts and a special commission appointed by Governor John C. Walton. The case was one of twelve flogging episodes in Oklahoma between November 1921 and July 1923. Charges were eventually filed against thirty-one citizens, all of whom admitted membership in the Ku Klux Klan.[39]

The Klan in Texas

The Klan was deep-rooted in Texas. By 1924, its former imperial kligrapp, Hiram Evans of Dallas, had become imperial wizard, the national commander of the Knights of the Hooded Order. Throughout the state, the warnings were clear as to what might happen to negroes who became too "uppity." Grand Titan H. C. McCall, head of the Houston Klansmen, personally led a mob of his hooded brethren to capture and castrate a negro dentist, Dr. J. L. Cockrell. He had been accused of associating with white women.[40]

In Dallas, in 1921, Imperial Kligrapp Evans himself had been the leader of a masked band which dragged bellhop Alex Johnson from a Dallas hotel. Accused of making improper remarks to white women, Johnson was acid-branded with a K-K-K across his forehead, presumably a warning to all others that they should henceforth keep their place.[41] In one of his speeches, Evans had said, "Every instinct, every interest, every dictate of conscience and public spirit, insist that white supremacy shall be forever maintained." Official Klan lecturer R. B. Sawyer went further, "The negro, in whose blood flows the made desire for race amalgamation, is more dangerous than a maddened wild beast, and he must and will be controlled."[42]

The climax of Klan triumphs in Texas seemed to be the activities of October 23, 1923, when Klan Day at the Texas State Fair in Dallas was officially proclaimed by State Fair officials. Some 75,000 Klansmen and their families from Texas and surrounding states attended the fair that day, and in the evening some 25,000 gathered for ceremonies in front of a gigantic flaming cross, the well-known Klan symbol. As a part of the day's activities the Klan donated to the people of Texas Hope Cottage, an institution for the care of homeless children, and one of the many worthwhile charities promoted by the Ku Klux Klan.[43]

The Klan in El Paso

While the Klan was reaching the zenith of its power in Dallas in 1923, it was definitely on its way downhill in El Paso. In April 1922, the Klan came through with a startling April Fool joke on those who had looked upon the organization as a small group of wild eyed super-patriots. In an El Paso school board election, three candidates for the board were clearly and openly the candidates of the Ku Klux Klan. The *El Paso Times*, which was the chief voice of the anti-Klan movement, backed two of its directors and another prominent citizen in opposing the Klan candidates. The total vote in the April 1 school board election was 10,819. It would be a good-sized school board vote even today, and all three of the Klan candidates were elected. Throughout 1922, the Klan openly celebrated its victory. Crosses burned on Mount Franklin and off the Newman Road, while the Klan prepared to run its candidates for county offices in the 1922 Democratic Primary.[44]

The Klan secured some moderate successes in the 1922 El Paso County elections, and as noted earlier, virtually gained control of the Texas Legislature, while a governor acceptable to the Klan won the election to that office. Meanwhile, the Ku Klux Klan was laying its plans to gain control of the city government of El Paso. P. E. Gardner, an El Paso lawyer and hotel owner, was the candidate of the Klan. His opponent, supported by all three El Paso newspapers, was Senator Richard M. Dudley.[45] To make the mayor's race, Dudley gave up a promising career in state politics. He and R. Ewing Thomason had entered the race for the two legislative positions from El Paso in 1916. They were elected by a large majority as "Anti-Ring Candidates," opposing the political "ring" which had controlled El Paso for many years. They both had highly successful first terms, and in 1918, Thomason was chosen speaker of the House and Dudley was elected state senator. By 1923, Dudley was clearly one of the leaders of the Texas State Senate.[46] He was persuaded to run for mayor in order to beat the threat of Klan control.

A campaign marked by bitterness, mob action, and extreme rhetoric on both sides finally came to a climax on Saturday, February 24, 1923. The *Times* headline that day said: VOTERS TO

DECIDE TODAY IF EL PASO SHALL BE CRUCIFIED ON THE
FIERY CROSS OF KLANDOM. Voters in nine El Paso precincts
decided in favor of the Klan, but Dudley carried all the others and
was elected by 7,573 votes to 5,452. His entire slate of aldermen
went into office with him.[47] A month later, on April 4, another
school board election was held and this time three anti-Klan candidates were elected.[48]

Even though the Klan was failing politically, it maintained an
active feud with the newly elected mayor. Through 1923 and part
of 1924, it published a weekly newspaper, edited by C. L. Sirmans,
kligrapp of the El Paso Chapter of the Klan. The paper was first
called *The Frontier Klansman*, then *The Fiery Cross*, and finally
The Klan Kourier.[49] In its issue of October 19, 1923, the Klan
announced the purchase of 160 acres of land near the Newman
road, to be "beautified and made a place of pleasure for members
of the Klan and their friends. . . . A Klavern, which will seat several
thousand people will be builded, and a fiery cross which, when
lighted, can be seen throughout El Paso County is being planned.
. . . Mayor Dudley is reported to have made the statement that
after the next County election the fiery cross shall not blaze in El
Paso County. Would like to see him spit on this one and put it out."

Mayor Dudley, in late October, had accompanied El Paso
labor leaders to Portland, Oregon, in an effort to obtain the 1924
national convention of the American Federation of Labor for El
Paso. In its issue of October 19, 1923, the *Frontier Klansman*
reprinted an article from a Klan publication in Portland: "Their
chief bid for the convention is that Juarez is the rottenest, vilest,
most putrid sore on the American continent . . . a place where
liquid poison is dispensed to American visitors, where vice is ram-
pant and where human vultures prey upon decency and defy every
law of God and man. Yet, this is what Dudley and Moran have
to offer the delegates to the convention of the American Federation
of Labor."

El Paso was contesting with Detroit for the 1924 convention
and when the vote was taken on October 12, 1923, the results
were: El Paso 14,587, and Detroit 12,885.[50] Upon his return to El
Paso, William J. Moran, AF of L official, stated that the Klan
attack on El Paso had backfired badly, and was, in fact, the chief
factor in securing the 1924 convention for El Paso.[51]

As 1923 faded into 1924, the feud with Mayor Dudley was the chief thing the El Paso Klan had going for it. The three El Paso dailies and the Klan publications kept the issue hot. In one of its issues, the *Klan Kourier*, successor to the *Frontier Klansman* and the *Fiery Cross*, told of the Klan gathering on Independence Day, 1924: "The largest gathering of white people ever assembled in the southwest took place at Klan Park on the 4th of July, when thousands of Klansmen and Klanswomen with their friends celebrated that great day in American history. Music was furnished by the Peerless Klan Band. Cyclone Davis, that great orator, was at his best."

On July 26, as he prepared to present his poll-tax receipt at Precinct 9, Dr. L. A. Nixon must have been well aware of all the Ku Klux Klan activity in El Paso. On that very day, the Klan would be foremost in the minds of many voters. The most celebrated race, for governor of Texas, pitted Mrs. Miriam A. Ferguson against Judge Felix D. Robertson. Mrs. Ferguson was admittedly representing her husband, former Governor Jim Ferguson, who had been impeached and was therefore ineligible to serve. While he did not admit it publicly, Judge Robertson, of Dallas, was clearly the candidate of the Ku Klux Klan. Two other candidates, both named Davidson, only served to confuse the issue. The battle was between Fergusonism and the Klan.⁵²

On the national scene, the Klan was drawing headlines in the press that same day. With ballots nearing the hundred mark, the Democratic National Convention was deadlocked in its choice for a presidential candidate. Meeting in New York's Madison Square Garden, the party was deadlocked between New York Governor Al Smith, vigorously opposed by the Klan because of his Catholicism and anti-prohibition sentiments, and William G. McAdoo, son-in-law of President Wilson. McAdoo was openly and strenuously supported by the Klan. The *El Paso Times* of July 26, 1924, reported that the Texas delegation had been loudly booed by the Smith faction because it failed to stand up to indicate opposition to the Klan. However, delegate R. Ewing Thomason, former speaker of the Texas House, and later to serve as mayor of El Paso, United States congressman and Federal district judge, wanted the press to record that he had stood up against the Klan.

The Nixon Challenge

If Dr. Nixon had read the Klan publications, he would have found little mention of negroes. It was easy to read between the lines, however, in an article in the *Frontier Klansman* of January 4, 1924, claiming that the Klan was responsible for a decrease in lynchings: "The fact is that the Ku Klux Klan is demanding and obtaining justice before the law for the negro, north and south. It is requiring white men to cease improper association with blacks, or suffer the same punishment from the law which the immoral negro receives. The Klan fights racial admixtures; it is adamant in its position in that regard." The message was clear: the negro would receive justice, so long as he kept his place.

Dr. Nixon encountered no spirit of hostility as he presented himself to election officials. As he recalled the event many years later, he said: "The judges were friends of mine. They inquired after my health, and when I presented my poll-tax receipt, one of them said, 'Dr. Nixon, you know we can't let you vote.'"

"I know you can't," Dr. Nixon replied, "but I've got to try."

"I've Got to Try"

What native impulses would give a little negro boy, born in Marshall, Texas, a life long obsession with the idea "I've got to try!"? There were many occasions when trying seemed hopeless in the face of restrictions placed upon people of minority races, but the record shows Dr. Nixon kept on trying.

The freeway, Interstate 20, has bypassed Marshall today, and as the traffic whizzes by some three miles distant, the city appears to have settled back into its historic splendor, its wide streets displaying proud southern mansions, fronted by gnarled and wide spreading trees. Active pioneer organizations will point out that, under the operations of the Confederacy, Marshall was the administrative capital of Missouri. Lieutenant Governor Thomas C. Raynolds moved to Marshall from Little Rock when a Federal advance threatened. He rented two houses, one labeled "Capitol of the State of Missouri," the other labeled "Governor's Mansion." Guides will point out the location of the Trans-Mississippi Agency of the Confederate Postal Service, the Confederate Ordnance Department for western operations, the Quartermaster and Commissary Departments, and a Confederate hat factory. The basement of the First Methodist Church of Marshall was used for the storage of Confederate military supplies.[53]

In a small city of such pronounced Confederate heritage, the opportunities for the negro, less than two decades after the Civil War, would be limited. That the negro was expected to keep his place was indicated by actions taken in 1881 to completely disfranchise all blacks in local elections of Harrison County, of which Marshall was the county seat.[54] This action was taken only three years before Lawrence A. Nixon was born in Marshall in 1884.

Nixon's Youth in Marshall

Despite many restrictions on the activities of people of his race, Lawrence Nixon must be presumed to have been born under relatively prosperous circumstances. His father, Charles Nixon, was chief steward, in effect the manager, of a luxurious private railroad car. Marshall had been a major distribution point for the Confederacy during the war, and its location made it a logical railroad center in the feverish railroad building era that followed the reconstruction period. Even before the war, the Memphis, El Paso and Pacific Railroad started laying its lines along the forty-mile stretch from Shreveport to Marshall, with the hope of building all the way to the Pacific to complete the nation's first transcontinental service. After the war, Jay Gould's financial empire gathered up the pieces of the Memphis, El Paso and Pacific and several other floundering roads and formed the Texas and Pacific Railroad, listing Marshall as the eastern-most point and heading westward across Texas with San Diego as the proposed western terminus.[55]

Jefferson, sixteen miles to the north from Marshall, and having better access to water transportation, had spurned Gould's offers. He indignantly wrote in the register of the Excelsior Hotel "the end of Jefferson." History-minded Jefferson residents have preserved the old hotel and proudly display Jay Gould's contemptuous statement. They have also managed to secure his luxurious private railroad car, the "Atalanta," [sic] with its four staterooms, lounge, kitchen, butler's pantry and bathroom.[56] The car was typical of the lavish expenditures by railroad tycoons in the 1870s and 80s.

Charles Nixon was chief steward of a perhaps equally lavish private car owned and operated by the general manager of the Texas and Pacific.

Move to New Orleans

There was busy rail traffic between Marshall and New Orleans, and when Lawrence Nixon was three the private car was moved to New Orleans. With it went the Nixon family, father, mother and four children. They were to stay in that prosperous and cosmopolitan southern city for the next five years. There is some indication of Charles Nixon's prosperity in the fact that he was able to send his children to a private school, instead of subjecting them to the inferior education offered in newly established segregated schools brought about by the reconstruction era. During these years, Lawrence Nixon had an English woman as his teacher. Her influence remained with him all of his life, for he never spoke with a typical southern accent, but a softly clipped manner of speech which caused people to believe he might be a native of the British West Indies.[57]

First Visit to El Paso

The Nixon family had the means not only for education but for travel, probably on railroad passes because of the father's employment. In 1894, Lawrence and his mother had an experience he was to remember the rest of his life. They boarded the Texas and Pacific in Marshall and traveled all the way across Texas to El Paso. Mrs. Nixon's brother was a barber in the fast-growing West Texas city, and they had come to pay him a visit. Dr. Nixon recalled in later years that they arrived during the rainy season and found the weather surprisingly cool and pleasant. Weather Bureau records for 1894 show only 4.24 inches of rainfall in El Paso for the entire year, but enough of it was concentrated in midsummer to give the Nixons a pleasant memory of a cool and invigorating climate. Lawrence was only ten years old, but the memory of that trip was to stay with him, and to influence the course of his life at a critical time, many years later.[58]

Back to Marshall

In the meantime, his education continued. In 1892, when he was eight, the family had moved back to Marshall, and he was enrolled in the teacher's training division of Wiley College. In this institution he was to continue his grade school, high school, and undergraduate college training.[59] Wiley is the oldest negro college west of the Mississippi, founded in Marshall in 1873, by the Freedmen's Aid Society of the Methodist Church. White men and negroes participated together in its founding, but one name among the founders would stand out in the memory of many a young negro at Wiley, the name of Meshach Roberts.

Meshach Roberts' Influence

"Shack" Roberts was a legend in Marshall. He was a giant of a man, in stature, in voice, and in influence among both races in the troubled days during and after the Civil War. He was a slave of O. B. Roberts and was brought to Gilmer, Texas, shortly before the war. While his master was serving in the Confederate Army, Shack operated the plantation. He was an excellent blacksmith, and worked for the neighboring plantations to earn money for seed. He also received payment in land and in the materials to build himself a cabin, and when he was given his freedom, he was in much better position than many newly freed blacks. But he took seriously the promises of political freedom and ran into difficulties with the Ku Klux Klan. He was beaten and left for dead beside a roadside near Gilmer. His former master cared for him, and induced him to move to Marshall.

In his new home, he became immediately active in the work of the Methodist Church, and the founding of Wiley College was but one of many services he performed to further the education of the large number of negroes in Harrison County. He also resumed his political activity and in 1873 he was elected to the first of three terms in the Texas State Legislature. Possessed of a strong voice, a rich gift of oratory, and a sharp sense of humor, he was considered one of the outstanding members of the House during the troubled reconstruction period.[60] With the complete disfranchisement of negroes in Harrison County following reconstruction,

Roberts dropped out of public life, but certainly his name would be remembered at Wiley College, and generations of negro boys who attended there would feel the hope that they, too, might make some contribution to the political freedom of their race.

Although Lawrence Nixon enjoyed unusual advantages, he still found it necessary to work if he expected a college education. His philosophy of work was expressed many years later, in 1952, in a letter to Walter White, national secretary of the National Association for the Advancement of Colored People:

My mother handled the family funds. She knew how to stretch a dollar. She made clothes and hats for herself and my sisters, red flannel underwear and pants from my father's discarded ones for me. I did not like to wear the pants because they were too tight, and very often the seat would rip when I stooped to stop a grounder while playing baseball. My mother loved flowers and, after we moved back to Marshall, she grew the most beautiful flowers I have ever seen.

I can't imagine a more happy childhood than my two sisters, my brother and I lived. We came up knowing how to work. A great deal of the joy of my boyhood came out of the work I did. My father disliked people who were ashamed to work with their hands.[61]

A Student at Nashville

At fourteen, Lawrence Nixon became an apprentice cabinet maker in the shops of the Pullman Company in Marshall, and worked there weekends and summers. During these years, he began to dream of becoming a physician and looking into the possibilities of a medical education. Two negro colleges had begun offering medical degrees before the end of the nineteenth century. There were the prestigious Howard University in Washington, D. C., and a lesser known but highly recommended school, Meharry Medical College, in Nashville. Lawrence chose the Tennessee school.[62]

Meharry Medical College had been established in 1876 as the Medical Department of Central Tennessee College. In 1900, the parent school became known as Walden University, and when Nixon enrolled there in 1902, it was known as Meharry Medical College of Walden University. In 1915, Meharry received a separate charter.[63] To pay his way through his final years at Wiley and his medical training at Meharry, Lawrence secured work as a Pullman porter, working from Chicago to San Francisco. He also found it necessary to work one summer at a Chicago bar.[64]

A Doctor at Cameron

In 1906, he returned proudly to Marshall as Dr. Lawrence A. Nixon. Pullman steward Charles Nixon and his wife did well in educating their children. Of the four, only one failed to receive a college degree. Lawrence, with his new medical diploma, began looking around for a place to practice, and sometime in 1907, he decided upon Cameron, the county seat of Milam County in the Brazos valley, some fifty miles southeast of Waco. Apparently his medical practice began well, for sometime during its earliest years, he returned to Marshall to marry a childhood sweetheart, Esther Calvin, the daughter of a Methodist minister. On July 4, 1909, their son Lawrence Joseph Nixon was born.[65]

Today, an urban renewal project has torn up much of the heart of Cameron, but on the south side of its old public square, the Milam County Courthouse still stands, built in 1892, and fronted by a statue of Ben Milam, hero of the Battle of San Antonio in the War for Texas Independence in 1835. Across the square from the courthouse stands a two-story building, also constructed in 1892. It has stores and offices on the ground floor, and a stairway entrance leading to the back of the second floor. This building answers Dr. Nixon's description of the site where he set up his first office, at the back of the second floor, in 1907. Late in that same year occurred a tragedy which was to sear his memory for the rest of his life, and intensify a search for greater freedom and human rights.

As the El Paso physician recalled the incident many years later, a negro named Alex Johnson was working as a shoe-shine man in Cameron and was generally well liked by people of the town. But in November 1907, a white girl claimed a negro had attempted to rape her, and Alex Johnson was taken into custody and charged with the crime. On the night of November 4, a mob dragged Johnson from his jail cell and killed him in the public square. Dr. Nixon remembered that chairs were placed on the balcony of the two-story building to accommodate the crowds gathered to witness the lynching, while the young doctor stayed behind locked doors in his office, listening to the cries of the dying man. According to Nixon's account, Alex Johnson was burned at the stake.[66] Accounts in both the *El Paso Times* and the *New York Times* for November 5, 1907, say the man was hanged from one of the trees in the courthouse yard.

Press reports could have been incorrect, or Dr. Nixon's memory could have been faulty. There were many lynchings to be remembered, 493 of them in Texas between 1882 and 1951.[67] A press summary showed seventy lynchings in the nation in 1909 alone, described as the highest number since 1904. The *El Paso Times* reported that "crimes or alleged crimes against white women, and murders, caused most of the executions." Georgia led the list with eleven and Texas followed with ten. Some of the specific "crimes" for which negroes were executed were: Martinsville, Louisiana, negro accused of counterfeiting; Hope, Arkansas, negro insulted white woman; Dawson, Texas, negro insulted white woman; Leighton, Alabama, negro accused of incendiarism; Barwick, Georgia, negro found hiding under the bed in the home of a white family; Clarksdale, Mississippi, negro accused of being concerned in a murder committed by his brother; Wallston, Georgia, negro caught peeping into a white woman's window.[68]

Burning at the stake was not unknown. In a summary of thirty years of lynching in the United States, the National Association for the Advancement of Colored People reported:

> On May 25, 1912, Dan Davis, a Negro, was burned at the stake in Tyler, Texas, for the crime of attempted rape. There was some disappointment in the crowd and criticism of those who had bossed the arrangements, because the fire was so slow in reaching the Negro. It was really only ten minutes after the fire had started that smoking shoe soles and the twitching of the Negro's feet indicated that his lower extremities were burning, but the time seemed much longer. The spectators had waited so long to see him tortured that they begrudged the ten minutes before his suffering really began.
>
> "I wish some of you gentlemen would be Christian enough to cut my throat," the victim said. There was no response. His last words were "Lord, have mercy on my soul."
>
> Some of the men and boys danced and sang to testify to their enjoyment of the occasion.[69]

On December 1, 1909, a negro preacher named John Harvard was driving his team of mules near Cochran, Georgia, when the team was frightened by an automobile driven by W. B. Booth. The two got into an argument and Harvard shot and killed Booth. A mob found the negro hiding in a barn. He was given an opportunity to pray and then bound to a stake with chains, the fuel was piled high above his head and the torch applied.[70]

One can hardly wonder that, in the perspective of the years, Dr. Nixon might have been confused as to just what happened in the public square beyond his locked door on that day in November 1907. Lynchings, whether hanging, shooting, or burning at the stake, were a way of life in much of America. The practice was widely defended. As late as 1918, a Maryland writer, Winfield H. Collins, wrote:

The Negro, child of Africa, but lately removed from the jungle, because of the necessity of the habitat of his origin, has had developed in him by nature, possibly stronger sexual passion than is to be found in any other race. But he is infinitely lacking in the high mental, moral, and emotional qualities that are especially characteristic of the Anglo-Saxon, and it is a grievous mistake to attribute such high qualities to him. When proper restraint is removed from the Negro, he gets beyond bounds. The Anglo-Saxon, indeed, or members of that race, has a way of meeting extraordinary conditions with extraordinary means—hence lynching in order to hold in check the negro in the South.

A mode of punishment that would be out of place as to the white man may well be suited to the Negro. Barbarous criminals require barbarous laws. The innocent and law abiding citizens of a State have rights as well as the criminals. But let some crafty scoundrel finally get in jail and he will be flooded with letters of consolation and sympathy from sentimental women and soft headed men. And let some Negro brute, guilty of rape, suffer the punishment he so richly deserved at the hands of an outraged community, and one would think, if he considered the bitter censure from distant quarters, that the foundations of the government were being undermined, or that a poor lamb was set upon by a pack of howling wolves, thirsting for blood, but not a word of commisceration for the family, or the victim, or the fiendish negro's unbridled bestiality.[71]

With such sentiments widespread, it should not be surprising that negroes would fear being arrested, even on the most trivial charges. In Rosebud, Texas, on December 20, 1909, less than three weeks after the widely publicized burning at the stake of the negro preacher in Georgia, a negro named Cope Mills was being arrested by a peace officer on a relatively minor charge. He tried to escape, there was an exchange of gunfire, and he shot and wounded the peace officer. Mayor Ward, of Rosebud, took up the chase, there was another exchange of gunfire, and the negro was wounded and captured. That night, a mob stormed the jail, took him to the fire station and hanged him from the fire house tower.[72]

Rosebud is only sixteen miles from Cameron, and two lynchings in the area in a period of two years caused Dr. Nixon to seek a safer place to practice his profession. He remembered the trip to El Paso with his mother twenty-five years earlier. El Paso was not a southern city, and he had hopes conditions there might be far better.

Move to El Paso

On December 31, 1909, Dr. Nixon and a good friend, Le Roy White, loaded the doctor's household and office furniture and his horse and buggy into one end of a freight car, took their bed rolls and a small stove into the other end, and set out on a ten-day journey to El Paso. Both were to spend the rest of their lives in El Paso. Le Roy White was for many years a government employee at the Stanton Street bridge, and served as assistant pastor of the Shiloh Baptist Church.[73]

On their long and tiring trip across Texas, Nixon and White might have been cheered if they had read some editorial comments in their future home. Concerning the burning at the stake in Georgia, the *El Paso Times* said:

There can be nothing but condemnation for the act of the Georgia mob which burned a Negro at the stake because he shot and probably fatally wounded a white man.

Granting that the Negro was entirely to blame, and that he murdered the white man without provocation, he was entitled to a trial, and upon conviction a legal execution. No sophistry, no distortion of the facts, no state of facts, can be pleaded in extenuation of the hideous and atrocious crime of the mob.

It is the actions of such infuriated mobs that bring reproach upon the south and subject our people and our civilization to misrepresentation and unjust condemnation, because they are accepted as acts of persons respresentative of the sentiment of Southern people. No one can defend it, and all right thinking people, regardless of sectional divisions, must condemn it, and unite in demanding the infliction of the severest penalties of the law against the perpetrators.[74]

A week later, on December 9, the *Times* headed another editorial "Mobbing by Courts or Lynching by Mobs":

Our dispatches told Tuesday night of a Negro rapist having been caught, tried, convicted and sentenced to death by a Kentucky court, all within a few hours.

This is generally considered swift justice, and is from one point of view, but in its last analysis it is lynching by the court, and is a recognition by the court of the strength of the claim set up by the mob in justification of lynching that the crime demands immediate and certain expiation, and of the two we prefer lynching by the mob to mobbing by the court, in that the former is not so far reaching in its consequences as the latter. The former is illegal, while the latter is sanctioned by law. The former reflects upon our citizenship and civilization, while the latter reflects upon the judiciary, and our whole system of jurisprudence. And there you are.

Treatment of the race problem by the El Paso press was not perfect; the *El Paso Herald* used the headline "Black Brute Murders Three" above the story of a triple murder in Savannah, Georgia, even though the second paragraph of the story beneath the headline told how one of the victims, a white woman, had regained consciousness long enough to implicate her husband, and he had been placed under arrest. Nevertheless, as far as Dr. Nixon was concerned, the move to El Paso was a move to a new atmosphere of freedom.

He found the public schools segregated, as they were all over Texas. He found that most restaurants denied him service, that most theatres and other places of entertainment refused him admission, and that there were many parts of the city where he could neither buy nor rent a home. Year after year, his application for membership in the El Paso County Medical Society was turned down, not because of any lack of medical qualifications but because he was black. A good friend, Dr. B. F. Stevens, tried in vain to sponsor his membership, and did make it possible through his sponsorship for Dr. Nixon to treat patients at El Paso hospitals.[75]

El Paso physicians pointed out that a requirement for membership in the El Paso County Medical Society was membership in the Texas Medical Association. That organization had long had in its constitution the word "white" as part of its requirements for membership.[76]

Offsetting in large measure the burdens of these handicaps was the privilege of doing something about such conditions, and knowing he would have the assistance of men and women of good will in both races. In 1910, when the National Association for the Advancement of Colored People was organized nationally, Dr. Nixon joined with L. W. Washington, Le Roy White and others to give El Paso one of the early chapters of the organization. The organization was welcomed by whites and negroes alike, and several white men and women became members.[77]

Dr. Nixon's El Paso Practice

Despite racial restrictions, his medical practice prospered. He located his first office at 101 South Campbell Street, just across the street from the courthouse. This location may have been partly responsible for an active interest in politics throughout the rest of his life. In 1923, he purchased a building for his home and office at 2029 Myrtle Avenue, an attractive site with a Japanese garden in the rear. He was instrumental in securing the site next door for building the Myrtle Avenue Methodist Church. The family had been active Methodists all of his years and he was trustee and choir member of the El Paso church.

Not all was happiness and success in those early El Paso years. He found his medical knowledge and the aid of his many friends to be powerless to save the life of his first wife, Esther Calvin Nixon, who died in the flu epidemic that claimed thousands of American lives in 1918. But even such bereavement might have worked its measure of good. Without a wife, and with his young son cared for by other members of the family, he was free to act in behalf of his people politically, without the thought that his own family might be endangered.

He voted regularly, and more important to his future and that of his race, he participated in politics as a member of the Democratic party. He was thus able to fill all the needed qualifications when the NAACP began looking for someone to test the 1923 Texas law which said that "in no event shall a negro be eligible to partici-

pate in a Democratic primary election held in the State of Texas."
He was an active Democrat, a regular voter, a charter member of
the NAACP. He had funds to help the expensive lawsuit ahead of
him and his people, he was free to act, and he was not afraid.

Results of His Vote Denial

He was the right man, in the right place, at the right time.
After he had been turned away from the voting precinct on July
26, 1924, an action was filed in his name in the United States
District Court, Western District of Texas, by El Paso attorney Fred
C. Knollenberg.[78] The complaint asked damages from election
judges C. C. Herndon and Charles Porras for denying L. A. Nixon,
"a qualified negro," the right to vote as guaranteed by the constitutions of both the United States and the State of Texas. The petition
stated that:

In El Paso County, in the State of Texas, the selection of candidates
in the Democratic Primary, for all practical purposes, determines the
officers who shall be chosen at the general election which will be held
in November, that for many years every officer in El Paso County has
been elected on the Democratic ticket and that they have no substantial
opposition from any other party.

That the opportunity to cast his ballot and to participate in this
election will pass with this date, to wit, Saturday, July 26, 1924, but the
rights which he now asserts herein are fundamental in their nature and
will continue as long as our system of laws prevail, and relator earnestly
prays that the court may consider this application, not only in the light
of the present Primary election, but in the light of the vast number of
people of his race and color who are vitally interested in the welfare of
their state and nation who look to the tribunals created by the constitutions of this state and nation to safeguard the rights and privileges which
those constitutions and laws have recognized and established.

Fred C. Knollenberg, Legal Counsel

When Dr. L. A. Nixon and the National Association for the
Advancement of Colored People turned to the courts to secure the
rights of negroes to vote in the Democratic primaries of Texas,
their choice of a lawyer to open the case in the El Paso Federal
District Court was a logical one, perhaps an inevitable one. Fred

C. Knollenberg was not only Nixon's personal attorney; he was the attorney to whom most negroes of El Paso looked at a time when few lawyers of the city were interested in representing them.[79]

The circumstances that had brought him to El Paso and into the Nixon cases were not of a planned nature, and could not in any way be described as a fulfillment of any long-term ambition. Fred Knollenberg was not even sure he wanted to become a lawyer. Born January 10, 1877, in Quincy, Illinois, he grew up associating with his father in the Knollenberg Milling Company. Quincy, on the Mississippi River, had a strong tradition of Republicanism; it had been the site of one of the Lincoln-Douglas debates. The Knollenberg family was Republican, and Fred continued as an active member of the party in El Paso, even while protesting in the courts that "in El Paso County . . . the selection of candidates in the Democratic Primary, for all practical purposes, determines the officers who shall be chosen at the general election which will be held in November."[80]

Fred C. Knollenberg was first educated as an accountant, preparing for his Certified Public Accountant examination at an accounting school in Quincy. It may have been a desire to handle tax matters more effectively which caused him to enter the Law School of the University of Michigan, where he received his LL B degree in 1901, at the age of twenty-four. Throughout his El Paso career, he took little part in criminal cases, and aside from his work in behalf of the franchise for negroes, his legal career was occupied chiefly with tax matters. In the years immediately following his graduation from law school, he seemed to have no desire to practice law, and resumed his association with the Knollenberg Milling Company.[81]

About 1907, during a fishing trip on the Mississippi, he suffered an attack of malaria, and was advised by his doctor to find a climate where malaria was not prevalent. He decided first upon the Rocky Mountain area, and then chose the southern part of the rockies as a more agreeable climate. Thus, in 1907, he came to Alamogordo, New Mexico. Unforeseen circumstances again shaped his career when he was urged, in Alamogordo, to assist mining companies in the Silver City area with legal problems pertaining to a series of labor disputes. It was in the Silver City area that he became acquainted with Judge Numa Frenger of Las Cruces, who urged him to pursue a legal career in the fast-growing community of El Paso. In 1910, the same year in which Lawrence A. Nixon came to El Paso to practice medicine, Fred C. Knollenberg arrived, passed the Texas bar examination, and began to practice law.

Knollenberg was a large man, six feet tall and 200 pounds, with a mouth full of gold teeth. This was the result of an accident as a newspaper carrier boy, when he fell off a trolley car, breaking all of his front teeth. Another boyhood accident had more serious consequences; a fireworks explosion cost him the sight of one eye. This encumbrance served only to make him work harder, and in his El Paso years, he was known as a lawyer who was always on the job. His work was never confined to office hours, and he was usually ready to see a client at any hour, day or night. A hearty, jovial man, a lovable family man, with a rich sense of humor; these are some of the qualities the family remembers about Fred C. Knollenberg, twenty-two years after his death in 1951.[82]

This was the Republican lawyer who, over a period of eight years, was to represent the claim of Lawrence A. Nixon and all other negroes of Texas to vote in Democratic primary elections. But other political parties might be involved to the same extent as the Democrats, and other races and groups to the same extent as negroes. As Knollenberg later argued before the Supreme Court:

> It is self-evident that if the Legislature of Texas in 1923 had the power to exclude the negro from the Democratic Primary, the Legislature of this or any other state, has the power to exclude him from the Republican primary. True, there is no useful purpose to be served in Texas in doing so; but if Texas has such power, all the other states likewise have it. If Maryland, New York, Pennsylvania, Massachusetts, or any other state should enact statutes excluding negroes, or any other class of citizens from the primaries of both Democratic and Republican parties would anyone have the hardihood to say such acts were valid? And yet the negro could not thereby more effectively be barred from participating in the choice of the governing officials than he is by the present Act of the Texas Legislature.[83]

Once the decision was made to employ Fred C. Knollenberg and his associates to file the case on behalf of Dr. Nixon, there arose the question as to what kind of case should be filed, and who it should be filed against. While it was recognized that the voting precinct judges were only carrying out the orders of the

party, and complying with a state law, it was nevertheless agreed
that the surest way to get the case before the Supreme Court for
definitive action was to file a suit against the persons who actually
denied Dr. Nixon the voting privilege. The judges were therefore
requested to sign a statement which became exhibit "A" in the
case of *Nixon v. Herndon and Porras*: "This is to certify that we,
C. C. Herndon and Charles Porras, Presiding and Associate Judge
respectively, have not permitted L. A. Nixon and J. H. Dudley to
vote as per instruction 26, given in ballot boxes to election hold-
ers."[84] J. H. Dudley was another negro denied the right to vote on
the same day.

As to what kind of case should be filed, Knollenberg later
explained in a letter to Walter White, then assistant secretary of
the NAACP in New York, that it was necessary to sue for damages,
since previous cases (*Chandler v. Neff*, and *Love v. Griffith*) had
indicated that action asking an injunction or a mandamus affirma-
tive action became a moot question on the day after the election.
"However," Knollenberg wrote, "I am not going to enforce collec-
tion of any sums of money against the defendants, who are innocent
victims of a vicious law, the only object of the suit being to get
an adjudication by the Supreme Court of the legal question."[85]

The Legal Fight Begins

The case filed in the District Court of the United States for
the Western District of Texas, sitting at El Paso, July 31, 1924,
therefore claimed: "That the aforesaid action of the defendants
herein was to plaintiff's damage in the sum of $5,000. Wherefore,
plaintiff prays for process in terms of law, and for judgment against
the defendants in the sum of $5,000, together with costs of this
suit." The petition was signed by L. A. Nixon and by attorneys
Fred C. Knollenberg and Robert J. Channel.[86] Channel and another
Knollenberg associate in El Paso, E. F. Cameron, were to appear
as co-counsels in the two Nixon cases, but clearly the chief counsel
was Knollenberg.

In the petition, Dr. Nixon's attorneys relied heavily upon the
protection of the fifteenth amendment to the Constitution, which
specifically directs itself to the subject of voting. As will be noted

later, the Supreme Court decision did not go into this aspect of the case, but the plaintiff's original petition made voting the dominant issue:

> . . . there are in the State of Texas two great political parties, the Democratic party and the Republican party; that by its terms, said act applies only to the Democratic party and does not apply to the Republican party; that the effect of such act is to exclude all negroes from participation in the Democratic primaries, forcing them, by implication to vote, if at all, only in a Republican primary; that said Act thereby discriminates as between the Democratic and the Republican parties and attempts by a legislative enactment to determine the party with which a negro shall affiliate, and deprives him of his rights as an American citizen to determine for himself his choice of parties, that such act is discriminatory interference with the free exercise of privileges of citizenship and suffrage enjoyed by the plaintiff, together with others of his race, similarly situated and conditioned in the State of Texas.[87]

An amendment to the original petition was filed October 7, 1924, citing Texas laws which, it was claimed, would also nullify the effect of the statute preventing negroes from voting in Democratic Primaries. On October 17, the defendants, represented by W. H. Fryer and R. E. Cunningham, members of a prestigious El Paso law firm, filed a motion to dismiss the case. The motion went directly to what seemed to be the central question—is a primary an election? Fryer and Cunningham believed not: "The petition shows that the primary election referred to was not an election within the meaning of the Constitution of the United States." Further, the defendants' lawyers charged that "the subject matter of the suit being political in nature, this court is without jurisdiction to determine the issues involved, or to award the relief prayed for."[88]

In a brief supporting the motion the defense tried further to place primary elections in a different perspective:

> A primary election has taken the place of a convention. . . . Therefore, in the event conventions were still in use, and a negro was denied a seat in the Democratic convention by the Democratic party, could it then be consistently maintained that the courts could force the Democratic Convention, a political party, to seat the negro? We contend that a primary election is purely a political matter, and this court has no jurisdiction in the matter.

Therefore, the lawyers argued, only authorized representatives of the Democratic party could complain, and Dr. Nixon was not a proper party to the suit. The defending attorneys quoted from a Supreme Court case, *Chandler v. Neff,* that primaries were unknown at the time of the fourteenth and fifteenth amendments: "Moreover, they are in no sense elections for an office, but merely methods by which party adherents agree upon candidates whom they intend to offer and support for ultimate choice by all qualified electors."[89]

This argument was assailed by the plaintiff's brief, filed by Knollenberg on November 5, quoting the statutes passed by Congress in support of the fourteenth and fifteenth amendments:

> Every person who, under color of any statute, ordinance, regulation, custom, or usage of any State or Territory, subjects, or causes to be subjected, any citizen of the United States, or other person within the jurisdiction thereof to the deprivation of any rights, privileges, or immunities secured by the Constitution and Laws, shall be liable to the party injured in an action at law, suit in equity, or other proper proceeding for redress.
>
> All citizens of the United States who are otherwise qualified by law to vote at any election by the people in any State, Territory, District, County, City, Parish, Township, School District, Municipality or other territorial subdivision, shall be entitled to vote at all such elections without distinction of race, color, or previous condition of servitude; any constitution, law, custom, usage, or regulation of any State or Territory, or by or under its authority, to the contrary notwithstanding.[90]

Clearly, questions of great national moment, requiring consideration by higher authority, were being raised in the Federal District Court at El Paso. On December 4, 1924, Judge Du Val West, then sitting in the San Antonio court of the Western District, sustained the defendants' motion to dismiss the suit, at the plaintiff's cost, without any explanation as to the merits of the case.[91] This action was expected by attorney Knollenberg, whose purpose from the beginning had been to get the issue before the United States Supreme Court by the shortest possible route. On February 27, 1925, Knollenberg and Channel filed an assignment of errors before the El Paso Court, asking the Supreme Court to reverse the dismissal.[92] On the same day, a petition for a writ of error was filed, and on the following day, Judge West granted an order that the case be heard before the Supreme Court on a writ of error. Knollenberg's strategy had worked, and the case would go directly to the high court, without intermediate action by a U.S. Court of Appeals.[93]

On to the Highest Court

In preparing the case for the Supreme Court, Knollenberg had the cooperation of the able executive and legal staffs of the National Association for the Advancement of Colored People. James Weldon Johnson, already distinguished as an outstanding negro poet and a brilliant legal spokesman for his race, is shown on a 1925 letterhead as secretary of the NAACP, with Walter White as assistant secretary. President of the association was a white man, a leading Boston lawyer, Moorfield Storey. The list of vice presidents included a leading New York lawyer, Arthur B. Spingarn, chairman of the association's Legal Committee, and such reformers as *New York Evening Post* Editor Oswald Garrison Villard and the Reverend John Haynes Holmes.[94] The Nixon cases were in every respect biracial efforts to establish political equality. The Nixon papers at the Lyndon Baines Johnson Library in Austin contain extensive correspondence between Fred Knollenberg and Moorfield Storey, James A. Cobb of Washington, Arthur B. Spingarn, and James Marshall.

Despite the assistance of such legal lights, the NAACP seemed to be often in financial distress, and Fred Knollenberg frequently found himself pleading for payment of his fees. In a letter to Assistant Secretary Walter White, dated January 30, 1925, he tried to clarify the agreement as to his payments:

When we started the case, I told the committee I would expect a fee of $2,000 for presenting the matter to the Supreme Court, and if I cannot give it the time and attention it deserves and get paid for giving it this time, I would prefer not to handle the matter. I will want to argue the case before the Supreme Court, and out of this fee will have to come my railroad fare and expenses to Washington, which will amount to approximately $500.

The question is of sufficient moment to every colored man in the United States that they could easily raise the money. If they are not sufficiently interested in their own case to do this, you cannot ask me to take my time to take up the matter from a purely sentimental standpoint.

In the same letter, Knollenberg asked an additional $500 to cover court costs, explaining: "We do not wish to be in a position where we will be compelled to use any part of our fee for this purpose, as I want to pay all costs as we go along. If they will give me half of it, and the Association will guarantee the payment to me of the other half within, say, six months, this will be satisfactory."[95]

Upon receipt of each letter concerning fees or expenses, Secretary Johnson or Assistant Secretary White would assure Knollenberg that the request had been referred to the Legal Committee for prompt action. Nevertheless, continued reminders of payments due are found throughout the Nixon papers. On October 29, 1925, Knollenberg wrote to White: "Up to the present time, we have received $500, and there is a balance of $1,500 due. . . . We are in default with the bank, and I wish it could be convenient to forward $380.00 so we can put it on deposit there and keep our word good." On November 29, 1926, he wrote: "Thanks for the $500 check to apply on fees—but it was not countersigned. I sure need the money, and I hate like the dickens to have it come back." In that same month, a letter to James Weldon Johnson said: "While we are on the subject, I wish you would tell your treasurer I am awful poor and need money so doggone bad I can taste it. Hope it will be convenient for you to send the balance of my fees some time between now and the middle of December, as I want to leave here about that time, and make a visit to Southeast Texas on the way to Washington."[96]

Knollenberg's financial problems were aggravated by ill health. He was evidently ill from mid-April 1925, until early July. Writing from Cloudcroft, New Mexico, on June 20, he told his associate, R. J. Channel: "I notice La Follette died from about the same thing and it sure makes a fellow think." Evidently Channel did not share Knollenberg's admiration for "Fighting Bob" for he replied: "As for La Follette, that fellow had it coming to him. Don't worry because he happened to select a method of departure somewhat similar to the little problem that has pestered you. When you reach his stage, methods will be unimportant. If it isn't one thing it's another. A fellow's resistance finally wears out. His had. Yours hasn't. And don't get impatient. I lost ten years, but I have come back fairly strong, best wishes." [97]

The Case Is Set

Knollenberg was soon back in action, and on October 12, 1925, he was able to wire the NAACP office in New York that the Supreme Court had set the case for the October term of court in 1926. The Association hurried to make a press release stating that the case of *Nixon v. Herndon* "will be made the entering wedge of an attack upon the disfranchisement of negroes in the South."[98]

Within a few months, Texas would be in another state election year, and once again Dr. Nixon would present himself at the polls in an attempt to vote in a Democratic Primary. He knew he would be refused again, but Knollenberg saw an opportunity to use the expected refusal as a vehicle to advance the case, hoping to secure a decision before the primary. He wrote the proposal to the NAACP Washington Counsel James A. Cobb, and in May 1926, he extended a trip eastward for the reunion of his graduating class at the University of Michigan to include a trip to New York and Washington where he conferred with NAACP officials and counsel. While in Washington, he and Cobb formally filed the motion to advance with the Supreme Court. On June 26, the motion was granted, but to no purpose since the case was merely advanced from January 18, 1927, to January 3.[99] By that time, of course, the Democratic primaries throughout Texas had already denied the voting privilege to negroes for the second time.

Knollenberg must have looked toward his first Supreme Court appearance with trepidation. He had to be told by Supreme Court clerk F. C. Stansbury that it would be necessary for him to apply for admission to the Bar of the Supreme Court before making an appearance. He requested the necessary forms for applying "together with any information which a green country lawyer should possess prior to making the application." He asked Cobb for some guidance as to when the case might actually be called, on January 3 or some indefinite date thereafter. "You understand of course that I am as green as grass with respect to their procedure, but I did not want to come up and stay in your infernal winter climate any longer than I just have to in January, so if we are set about the heel of the docket, you could give me rather an idea when we will be called, and I will then punch the clock at that time."[100]

As the date for his appearance approached, however, he began to wonder if he had appeared too modest. In a letter to lawyer Moorfield Storey, president of the NAACP, he wrote:

> I want to correct a seeming impression that I made in my letter, for I have never before been accused of being bashful, nor having a retiring disposition, and I look forward with a great deal of pleasure to addressing the Supreme Court in this case, in which I have the utmost confidence, and wish to thank you for your suggestion with regard to the court, and in your absence will do the best I can to present our case and win it. And I thank you for the confidence expressed in your letter.[101]

As the time for the case approached, it became evident that no argument would be presented to the Supreme Court on behalf of defendants Herndon and Porras. Attorneys Fryer and Cunningham had earlier advised Knollenberg that they were no longer connected with the case, and Charles Porras, the defendant election judge, advised that he would not make any contest. The position of the court would be merely to decide whether or not Judge Du Val West had erred in dismissing, without trial, the case of *Nixon v. Herndon and Porras*. Knollenberg surveyed the case in a letter to Secretary James Weldon Johnson of the NAACP on November 18, 1926: " . . . wish to ask you if you don't want to come down . . . and hear the argument. I know it will be one sided, for the other folks have not filed a brief. However, under these circumstances it often times happens that the court represents the absent side, in which case I would be on the other side, which makes hard going." [102]

The case was called for argument on January 4, 1927, and the record shows Fred C. Knollenberg and Arthur B. Spingarn argued the case with a written brief submitted by Louis Marshall, Moorfield Storey, and Knollenberg's El Paso associate Robert J. Channel.[103]

Knollenberg's Appearance

In a letter to Moorfield Storey on January 20, Knollenberg described his first appearance before the Supreme Court of the United States:

The question being new and novel, the Court took me to task quite a little, and really the entire time allotted was used in answering questions propounded by different members.

The Chief Justice and Justices Holmes and Brandeis seemed to be in sympathy with our position, and I feel Justice Stone is as well. However, Justice Butler and Justice McReynolds took issue with me and judging from the position that they took in the argument, I feel that they will file a report adverse to our position. My only hope is that they do not write the majority opinion.

Mr. Spingarn discussed the Newberry case, as Justice McReynolds seemed to feel that it was binding upon us, and that the United States Government had no authority under the constitution over primary elections. When we had finished, Dan Moody, who was then Attorney General of the State of Texas and is now Governor, was in the court room waiting to present a case for the State of Texas, following ours, and he asked permission to file a brief. For if the court holds our position is good with respect to the primaries, he, of course was elected at a primary acting under a void law, and his nomination would be subject to attack.

The Court granted him the right to file a brief and gave us fifteen days in which to answer. I have asked Governor Moody to see that the brief is gotten to me as soon as possible, and as soon as I get it will forward it, together with a tentative reply, to yourself, to Mr. Arthur Spingarn, and to Mr. James A. Cobb, with the hope that you will finish it up in such a way that the court will see the Nixon case our way.[104]

As summarized by the Supreme Court in the *Nixon v. Herndon* decision, the brief submitted by Attorney General Claude Pollard for the State of Texas added nothing substantial to the arguments already made in the briefs to the El Paso District Court. Claiming that political questions are not within the province of the judiciary, the brief continued: "There can be no doubt that, so far as the law of Texas is concerned, the Democratic nominating primary held in El Paso in July 1924 was not an election in which the plaintiff in error had a constitutional right to vote."[105] Dr. Nixon's attorneys needed little new research to present an answer to material which was all too familiar.

The Decision Is Favorable

The decision of the Supreme Court was announced on March 7, 1927, and to the surprise of Fred Knollenberg the decision was unanimous, with Justice Oliver Wendell Holmes delivering the opinion of the court. After reviewing the facts of the case, Justice Holmes proceeded to the claim by the defendants and by the State of Texas, in its intervening brief, that the case was political and not within the jurisdiction of the court:

> The objection that the subject matter of the suit is political is little more than a play on words. Of course, the petition concerns political action, but it alleges and seeks to recover for private damage. That private damage may be caused by such political action, and may be recovered for in a suit at law, hardly has been doubted for more than 200 years.

The Justice here quoted numerous precedents for such recovery in suits at law, and the wisdom of filing a case against election judges for actual damages could be seen. Since damages were involved, it made no difference whether the election was a primary or general election: "If the defendants' conduct was a wrong to the plaintiff, the same reasons that allow a recovery for denying the plaintiff a vote at a final election allow it for denying a vote at the primary election that may determine the final result."

Still, Justice Holmes seemed to depart from the question of voting rights, and concentrate on the denial of equal rights under the law:

> We find it unnecessary to consider the 15th amendment because it seems to us hard to imagine a more direct and obvious infringement of the 14th. That amendment, while it applies to all, was passed, as you know, to protect the blacks from discrimination against them.
>
> That amendment not only gave citizenship and the privileges of citizenship to persons of color, but it denied to any state the power to withhold from then the equal protection of the laws. What is this but declaring that the law in the states shall be the same for the black as for the white, that all persons, whether colored or white, shall stand equal before the laws of the states, and in regard to the colored race, for whose protection the amendment was primarily designed that no discrimination shall be made against them by law because of their color.
>
> The statute of Texas, in the teeth of the prohibition referred to, assumes to forbid negroes to take part in a primary election, the importance of which we have indicated, discriminating against them by the distinction of color alone. States may do a good deal of classifying that is difficult to believe rational, but there are limits, and it is too clear for extended argument that color cannot be made the basis of a statutory classification affecting the right set up in this case.
>
> Judgment reversed.[106]

FRED C. KNOLLENBERG
The self-styled "green country lawyer" from El Paso
represented Dr. L. A. Nixon before the U. S. Supreme Court.
(Mrs. Robert Hoy)

JUSTICE OLIVER WENDELL HOLMES
"Color cannot be made the basis of a Statutory classification affecting the right set up in this case [Nixon vs Herndon]."
(Library of Congress)

JUSTICE BENJAMIN NATHAN CARDOZA
"The 14th amendment, adopted as it was with special solicitude for the equal protection of members of the Negro race, lays a duty upon the Court to level by its judgement these barriers of color."
(Library of Congress)

Mrs. Drusilla Tandy Nixon
*Dr. Nixon's widow holds the pen which Justice Oliver Holmes
used to write the Nixon vs Herndon decision and a certificate
from the Justice's secretary.*
(Millard G. McKinney)

It would be for future to determine whether the renowned Justice Holmes had left loopholes by not invoking the fifteenth amendment as well as the fourteenth, and by not saying flatly that the words "the right of citizens of the United States to vote" in the fifteenth amendment, included primaries as well as general elections. In the meantime, it was a heady victory for the "green country lawyer" Fred Knollenberg. Back home in El Paso, the Republican-leaning *El Paso Herald* said: "The decision, it is believed, has administered the greatest setback the Texas Democratic party has ever received." The story was given front page treatment on March 7, 1927, the day of the decision in Washington, and it began:

> What is regarded as the most significant case ever carried to the Supreme Court of the United States by an El Paso attorney was decided Monday morning in his favor when the Court held that the Texas law prohibiting negroes from voting in the Democratic Primary was unconstitutional. The style of the case was A. L. [*sic*] *Nixon vs C. C. Herndon*, et al, and it was carried to the Supreme Court by Fred Knollenberg. . . . The case was filed in the United States court here by Mr. Knollenberg after C. C. Herndon and Charles Porras, judges in the July, 1924 primary refused to permit L. A. Nixon to vote. . . . Local Democrats were admitting Monday that Mr. Knollenberg had stirred up a hornet's nest as far as their party is concerned.

The Quill Pen of Justice Holmes

Ever since the case was argued, Knollenberg had been confident of the outcome. On February 19, he had written William R. Stansbury, clerk of the Supreme Court:

> I have a peculiar request that I wish to make and was wondering if you would have any objections to having the Justice, who renders the decision in the case of Nixon vs Herndon, et al, to sign with one of your quill pens, which I would very much like to have, and would appreciate it if you would get it and mail it to me, as I feel it will be a memento that I should like to keep on account of the extremely broad and far reaching question involved in the case. To me, as just a country boy, it seemed surprising that the Justices so quickly caught the broad import of the question when it did not seem to have any effect at all with our local folks, who rather seemed to feel that it was an unimportant and merely a local question.

After the decision Knollenberg renewed the request for the
quill pen in a letter to Justice Oliver Wendell Holmes who wrote
the opinion:

I was indeed pleased to receive your wire today that decision in the
Nixon vs Herndon case was rendered by you, as I was very much interested
in the case; for it, according to my mind, involved a far reaching principle
that the other folks did not seem to appreciate. However, the question
seemed important to me, and as most country lawyers, I was very much
enthused with it.

I sent you a wire asking for a pen. The pen my clients desire to use, as
it marks another epoch in their rights for which they have been fighting.[107]

The pen, and the opinion autographed by Justice Holmes,
were framed and hung for many years in Knollenberg's office.
They are now in the possession of Mrs. L. A. Nixon.

If El Paso readers were curious as to who the A. L. or L. A.
Nixon in the case might be, they were not enlightened by the local
press. In none of the stories was his address given, nor was he
referred to as "Dr.," although he had been a reputable medical
practioner in the city for seventeen years.

On March 8, the day following the decision, both the *Herald*
and the *Times* were speculating about the actions that might be
taken by the legislature in Austin in response to the Supreme Court
action. The *Times* commented editorially: "The bulk of the negro
population of the south has been deprived of the vote, constitution-
ally, by shrewd local ruses." There would be more such ruses
before Lawrence A. Nixon and other negroes would be able to
enter the polling place in a state of equality with white voters.

Political Ramifications

In 1926, Dan Moody at age thirty-two was the bright young
man of Texas politics. As a prosecuting attorney who had crusaded
against the Ku Klux Klan, he had won a convincing victory as a
candidate for Texas attorney general in 1924. By the time he took
office in 1925, the Klan was well on its way out as an influence
in Texas politics, but Moody was able to capitalize on its downfall,
and in 1926 he was the logical choice as the Democrat to beat
Governor Miriam A. (Ma) Ferguson in the Democratic Primary,

and put an end to "Fergusonism," which, to many Texans, was a more dangerous enemy than the Klan had been. Admittedly, the governor was being directed in office by her husband, who was barred from seeking the office himself as he had been impeached by the legislature and removed from office. Moody's margin over Mrs. Ferguson in the first primary was more than 120,000 votes, but votes cast for four other candidates made a runoff necessary. In the second primary, Moody defeated Mrs. Ferguson 495,723 to 270,295.[108]

With all this political activity in 1926, he had little opportunity to know of an obscure case in the federal courts, dismissed by the Federal District Court, in which a negro had tried to vote in a Democratic primary. As reported earlier, Governor-elect Moody just happened to be in the Supreme Court, on another case, on the day when the Nixon case was argued. He may have realized suddenly that a victory by Dr. Nixon's lawyers would jeopardize his own hard-won victory in the two Democratic primaries. The courts might well hold that the primaries, having illegally denied the vote to negroes, were illegal and of no effect. Such a possibility certainly occurred to Fred Knollenberg. After interviewing him following Judge Holmes' decision, the *El Paso Herald* said: "Because of the verdict it is possible that all candidates nominated in Democratic primaries in this state may be placed in jeopardy." It is highly possible that Knollenberg was also responsible for alerting Governor Ferguson and her husband to this possibility. In the Nixon papers at the Lyndon Baines Johnson Library in Austin there is a copy of a letter dated January 15, 1927, eleven days after the Nixon case was argued in Washington. The letter is unsigned. There is no name at the bottom and no initials, but its appearance indicates it was written on the same typewriter as many of Knollenberg's letters. The files contain no reply to the letter, nor any indication it was ever received. Addressed to Honorable James E. Ferguson, Austin, Texas, it reads:

Dear Governor Jim:
    I just had a conference with Honorable Fred C. Knollenberg who argued the case of Nixon vs Herndon and others in the Supreme Court of the United States the other day, which questioned the constitutionality of our Primary Election Law insofar as the negroes were prohibited from participating in the Democratic Primary, and it just occurred to me that

if his position is sustained—and he thinks it is going to be, then Moody's nomination in the primaries was void, and if this is so, it would naturally show that Governor Ferguson was beaten by virtue of a void and unconstitutional law, and you should take some steps such as you may wish to protect the Governor in her office, until someone is duly elected and the law established and the Primary Election Statute held valid, and from reading the brief of Judge Knollenberg's, I am constrained to believe his position is tenable, and if so, it will knock Moody's nomination higher than a kite.

I am serious in this matter, and Moody, who was in Washington at the time Judge Knollenberg argued this case has permission of the Supreme Court to file a brief, and told the court that the election of the Governor of Texas might hinge on this law and that Jim Ferguson was liable at any minute to file proceedings against him to prohibit him from taking the Governorship of the State. I am confident there is something in this and at least enough in it to deal Moody a bunch of misery, and knowing you to be one of the best lawyers in Texas, I trust you can see the point involved, and I will take pleasure in sending you a copy of the Knollenberg brief and such other matters as you may think necessary in the premises.
. . . Any further information or service I can be to you, command me,

As ever yours,[109]

Attempts to Circumvent the Decision

Whether or not such a letter was ever mailed, it is clear that Governor Moody felt that some changes in the Texas Primary Election laws were urgently needed. The regular session of the Texas Legislature was nearing its close on March 7, when the *Nixon v. Herndon* decision was announced; it finally adjourned March 16, but a special session was called for May 9, 1927. The governor's call did not list corrective legislation on party primaries in his official call for the special session, but he left open action on "such other matters" as might be recommended during the progress of the session. On May 25, the governor sent a letter to "The Honorable Fortieth Legislature of the State of Texas," which was read to both chambers on the following day. Included in a list of recommended legislation was this:

The Supreme Court of the United States has held Article 3107, Revised Civil Statutes, 1925, is violative of a provision of the Constitution of the United States. I submit for your consideration the repeal of this article and the enactment of a statute which will vest power in the executive committee of the several political parties to determine the qualifications requisite to membership in such parties.[110]

Governor Moody, a good lawyer, had worded his recommendation carefully so a claim could not be made that its primary purpose was to disfranchise the negro. But a good lawyer scanning the House Journal would have little trouble discerning that such was the purpose. The bill was ready for introduction and was presented to the House on the same day by Representative Travis E. Smith of Smith County. Smith's effort was a loosely worded bill, soon to be discarded in favor of the Senate bill, but it passed the House on second reading the following day, on a vote of 83 to 17. Among those opposing it were Representatives Joseph McGill (later an El Paso County judge) and W. R. Poage of Waco (to become the powerful chairman of the Agriculture Committee in the United States House of Representatives). Also opposing the bill was Hubert T. Faulk of Quitman, Wood County. Years later, Faulk would be a well-known and controversial lawyer in El Paso.

Faulk told the House his reasons for opposing the bill:

> I voted against House Bill No. 57 because it confers too much authority on thirty-one members. I sought to amend the bill by providing that these thirty-one men shall never prescribe property holding as a qualification for voting. As passed, the act empowers the state executive committee to prescribe without limit the qualifications of a voter, and they have ample power under this act to say that a man must be a Methodist, a Mason, and a millionaire.
>
> This savors of autocracy, and I will not sanction it by my vote. I will support any reasonable bill to curb the negro vote.[111]

This action took place Friday and by Tuesday, May 31, the bill was finally passed and on its way to the Senate. McGill, Poage and Faulk were still in the opposition, but the most vigorous criticism was voiced by Representative A. R. Stout of Ennis, Ellis County:

> It is doubtful that the bill will accomplish its purpose in view of the recent holding of the Supreme Court of the United States. . . . Admitting for the sake of argument that it would do so, then I am not willing to turn my government over to a small number of men who compose the State Executive Committee.
>
> The South has always handled the "nigger" in a satisfactory manner and will continue to do so.
>
> I had rather take my chances on handling the "nigger" than I would on thirty-one men who would have final authority to determine who should vote and who should not vote, and who should be a Democrat and not be a Democrat.[112]

In the Senate, the bill was introduced by Senator R. S. Bowers, of Caldwell, the same senator who had introduced the bill denying negroes the vote in Democratic primaries, found unconstitutional by the Supreme Court. He was joined by Senator T. J. Holbrook, of Galveston. On June 1, the Senate received the House bill and promptly moved to substitute the language of its own bill. While the bill finally passed with a House number (H. B. 57), its final form was substantially as introduced by Senators Bowers and Holbrook. As finally passed and signed by the governor on June 7, the bill contained a clause which Fred Knollenberg would use before the Federal courts. What, he would ask, was the nature of the emergency in Section 2, other than to deprive the negro of the right to vote?

Be it enacted by the Legislature of the State of Texas:

Section 1. That Article 3107 of Chapter 13 of the Revised Civil Statutes of Texas be and the same is hereby repealed and a new article is hereby enacted so as to hereafter read as follows:

"Article 3107. Every political party in this State, through its state executive committee shall have the power to prescribe the qualifications of its own members and shall in its own way determine who shall be qualified to vote or otherwise participate in such political party; provided that no person shall ever be denied the right to participate in a primary in this state because of former political views or affiliations or because of membership or non-membership in organizations other than the political party."

Section 2. The fact that the Supreme Court of the United States has recently held Article 3107 invalid, creates an emergency and an imperative public necessity that the constitutional rule requiring bills to be read on three several days in each house be suspended, and that this act shall take effect and be in force from and after its passage, and it is so enacted.[113]

Retrial of Nixon's Case in El Paso

While the State Executive Committee of the Democratic Party prepared to take action under the new legislation, there was some unfinished business in El Paso regarding the *Nixon v. Herndon* case. The Supreme Court had merely reversed the decision of the Federal District Court in El Paso, which had dismissed the case. The case was therefore not dismissed, and had to be brought to the court for trial. The case was set for February 1, 1928, and a twelve-man jury, with Jake Kaufman as foreman, was chosen to hear the case. The verdict, returned the same day, said simply "We the jury under instructions of the court, find for the plaintiff, L. A. Nixon, against the defendants, C. C. Herndon and Charles Porras, in the sum of one dollar, Jake Kaufman, Foreman."

The judgment, filed February 1 by Judge Charles A. Boynton, said:

> The court doth find that the law and the evidence is with the plaintiff. ... Said refusal was a denial to the plaintiff of his rights, and that plaintiff is damaged, and the Court finds his measure of damages to be $1.00. It is therefore ordered, adjudged and decreed by the Court that the plaintiff, L. A. Nixon, have and recover of and from the defendants the sum of $1.00 and costs of suit for which let execution issue.[114]

Dr. Nixon, as the plaintiff, appeared in court for the trial and judgment, but defendants Herndon and Porras did not even put in an appearance, nor were they represented by counsel, Fryer and Cunningham having left the case before its hearing by the Supreme Court. As Knollenberg explained at the beginning of the case, no substantial damage case would be presented. The only purpose of asking damages was to get the case before the Supreme Court for a decision. In this, Nixon's attorneys had succeeded admirably.

The Next Election

The year 1928 was a presidential election year, and in Texas the Democratic Primary would choose from six candidates for the United States Senate and five candidates for governor. Voters of the sixteenth Congressional District, which included El Paso, would vote for two candidates for the United States House of Representatives. In each case, the winner of the Democratic Primary could be assumed to be the final winner. There would be no Republican Primary, the party having polled fewer than the required 100,000 votes in the previous gubernatorial election. Except for the election of the president, the Democratic Primary was the only election that mattered, and once again, the negroes of Texas would be denied the right to participate in it.

Well in advance of the primary, the Democratic State Executive Committee of Texas passed a resolution:

RESOLVED: That all white Democrats who are qualified and under the Constitution and Laws of Texas and who subscribe to the statutory pledge provided in Article 3110, Revised Civil Statutes of Texas and none other, be allowed to participate in the primary elections to be held July 28, 1928 and August 25, 1928, and further, that the Chairman and Secretary of the State Democratic Executive Committee be directed to forward to each Democratic County Chairman in Texas a copy of this resolution for observance.[115]

Long before any agreement was reached with the National Association for the Advancement of Colored People regarding another case for the Supreme Court, Fred Knollenberg was laying his plans. On June 20, 1928, he wrote Arthur B. Spingarn, chairman of the association's legal committee, enclosing a copy of the above resolution, and added: "Wish to ask what you think of it. From the reports here, the folks want to start another suit. This will necessarily have to be a little bit different from the other one, on account of the fact that we will be compelled to include in the suit the State Central Committee."[116]

Further Attempts to Gain Voting Rights

Evidently, it had not entered Knollenberg's mind that the NAACP legal staff would object to this strategy, and he began at once to put it into effect. On June 22, 1928, Dr. L. A. Nixon wrote identical letters to all members of the State Democratic Executive Committee. The letters were sent by registered mail with return receipt requested:

Dear Sirs:
    I notice that you and your associate members of the Democratic Executive Committee of Texas have fixed a qualification of voters in the coming Democratic Primary Election to be held on July 28, 1928, so as to allow only white Democratic voters and none others to participate which will unquestionably prohibit me, a duly qualified voter and tax-payer, but a negro, in aiding in the selection not only of the County, District and State officers, but also electors for President, Vice President and Congressmen and Senators of the United States. . . .

    Now, on behalf of myself, and the other duly qualified negro Democratic voters of the State of Texas, I respectfully demand that you and the members of the Democratic Executive Committee of the State of

Texas, amend your instructions so as to allow me, and all other qualified negro Democratic voters to participate in the Primary, or we will be compelled to enforce our rights in the Federal Court under Revised Statutes Sections 2004, 1979, 1980, which we think makes you personally liable, and in case we are denied the right to vote, I will file suit against you individually for damages caused by preventing me from exercising my right of franchise. . . .

You, of course, understand that we dislike to do anything of this sort and feel that your regulation is arbitrary and in violation of the law, and deprives the Democratic negroes in Texas of a very valuable right, and hope that you will amend your regulations so we may vote in the Primary.

Very truly yours,
L. A. Nixon

One of the letters was returned unclaimed, and the Nixon papers contain but one answer to the others. It came from a Wichita Falls attorney, Charles I. Francis:

I received your letter requesting that the Democratic Executive Committee allow you to participate in the ensuing primary wherein the Texas Democrats are selecting their candidates for State and National offices.

While I did not attend the meeting at Waco at which this qualification was fixed, I believe that the Committee acted in accordance with the provisions of the Texas law which was enacted pursuant to the decision of the United States Supreme Court in the Nixon case.

The Republican party of this state, aided by a few disgruntled Democrats, will doubtless be glad to have your co-operation and assistance in selecting their State and National candidates, as was true in the case of their selection of candidates for President and Vice President. The Republican party in its platform and through its Presidential nominee has made a bid for negro support, and it may be that the Republican policies are more in line with your ideas of government than are those of the Democratic party in Texas.

Charles I. Francis[117]

Successful as his first case had been before the Supreme Court, Knollenberg was evidently trying every possible angle to win the second case without a court battle. On June 15, 1927, he had written Governor Dan Moody:

Dear Governor Moody:
    I noticed in the papers that the Legislature passed some sort of an Act which, according to the press reports, is attempting to avoid the

effect of the decision of the Supreme Court in the case of Nixon vs Herndon. It seems to me as if this is all wrong, particularly in view of the fact that the Court kindly gave you the right to file a brief. I felt that when the bill was presented to you, since you were personally before the Supreme Court, you would scan it carefully so as not to be placed in the position, after having been favored by the Justices, of allowing a bill to pass to avoid the effect of the decision.

I have been trying to get a copy of the bill, but without success, and would appreciate it very much if you would furnish me with a copy, and I think I can give you some authority which will satisfy you that it is unconstitutional and give you the right to overrule the action of the legislature.

I will appreciate hearing from you at your convenience. . . .

His only answer was a letter from the governor's secretary stating that the governor had already signed the bill and filed it with the secretary of state. Following his unsuccessful letters to the members of the state executive committee, he appealed to their chairman, D. W. Wilcox, of Georgetown, Texas, to change the ruling "so as to allow the negro to vote."[118] Apparently this appeal went unanswered.

Back to the Courtroom

There was apparently no recourse but to go to court again, and both Knollenberg and the NAACP legal staff agreed that Dr. L. A. Nixon should be the plaintiff again. In a letter to Walter White, Knollenberg wrote: "Dr. Nixon as plaintiff cannot help but have a wonderful psychological effect upon the Court as he was compelled previously to go to the Supreme Court to try to vote in Democratic Primaries, and there was no question about his being a Democrat."[119] The NAACP agreed and again, on July 28, 1928, Lawrence A. Nixon presented his poll-tax receipt at the same East El Paso fire station and requested permission to vote. The election judges again turned him away, quoting this time the instructions of their state executive committee.

From this point on, there was a fundamental disagreement between Knollenberg and his associates of the NAACP legal staff as to how the case should be prosecuted. The Nixon papers include letters back and forth throughout the last halff of 1928, with Knollenberg insisting that the thirty-one state executive committee members, who made the decision, should be included, along with election judges James Condon and C. H. Kolle, among the defendants. In a letter to Arthur B. Spingarn, NAACP vice president and legal adviser, Knollenberg argued:

> . . . Now we think that we told you the foundation we have laid. In the first place, when they were getting ready to pass the new act, we wrote to Governor Moody, who, you remember, was granted special consideration by the Supreme Court when you finished your argument in order to file his brief, and we felt that it was in a measure showing disrespect to the Supreme Court to pass something to avoid the effect of their decision when they had given him special personal consideration.
>
> In the next place, we got the names of each one of the State Democratic Executive Committee, and registered a request signed by Dr. Nixon, asking them to retract their instructions allowing only white Democratic voters to participate in the Primary. Each one of these notices were delivered, and we have a registry receipt back in our files covering it. Our idea is to bring a suit for damages not only against the judge who refused Dr. Nixon the right to vote, but also the County Chairman who directly gave them the instructions, and each member of the State Executive Committee who promulgated the rules. This will compel them to come to El Paso from all parts of the State, and the eastern fellows are somewhere around 900 to 1,00 miles away, and as soon as we file the suit there are some of those fellows going to be mightly sore. Now just imagine yourself being placed in this position, and if they are at the next election members of the Committee, they will seriously consider it inadvisable to pass such damn fool instructions.[120]

The Strategy is Mapped

On November 9, 1928, William T. Andrews, special legal assistant of the NAACP, telegraphed Knollenberg to hold up papers "until we are able to send suggestions of Mr. Marshall." A letter from Andrews the next day made it clear that Louis Marshall of the firm of Guggenheimer, Untermeyer and Marshall was planning the strategy in the case, that Marshall was preparing a brief stating his theory on the constitutional questions involved and that

> He doubts the advisability of making various members of the Democratic State Committee parties defendant. He is of the opinion that there is no cause of action against the members of the committee and that making them parties, you lose sight of the true significance of the action. He says that the chances would be that the complaint would be dismissed,

as to each of the members of the committee, with costs, and that if each member of the committee were to appear by a different lawyer these costs might amount to a large sum.

Knollenberg Presses the Case

Knollenberg was willing to take that chance, and in his reply of November 13, he reminded the association that he had agreed to take the case for a fee of $2,500, with a maximum of $1,500 for costs. He would absorb any costs over the $1,500. He gave these five reasons for filing suit against the Democratic Executive Committee members:

1. The law, as passed, and which we must have construed as unconstitutional, gives them the right to decide the qualifications of the voters.
2. They had notice prior to the Primary that Dr. Nixon was demanding for himself and other negroes of the State of Texas, the recall of the resolution.
3. The demand was made by registered letter on each of them.
4. If we can't include the State Executive Committee, our remedy or recovery will be limited merely to a local affair.
5. If we bring a suit against the local judges, they can admit that they are wrong, submit it to a jury, and we will recover practically nothing.

Now, in closing, allow me to suggest that, of course, we appreciate the fact that Mr. Marshall is a big lawyer, and has reached a place at the Bar of the United States which we can never expect to reach, and we respect his judgment, but there are a great many lawyers, many of them in Texas, who said we could not put over the other suit, but we did it, and we feel we can do this the same way.[121]

Fred Knollenberg no longer characterized himself as a "green country lawyer." He had carried a highly significant case to the Supreme Court and won. He felt he had the right to talk plainly and forcefully to one of the top lawyers of the nation, and after reading Louis Marshall's detailed brief, he wrote him at 120 Broadway, New York, on March 5, 1929:

I am taking the liberty of addressing you personally, for we value the opinion of Mr. Louis Marshall as a great many lawyers in the United States do. Feeling as we do, we were of the opinion that the other view should be placed before you, prior to filing suit, to see whether or not it might have some bearing on the decision you have indicated in your letter.

In a five-page letter, he analyzed the forthcoming case, and on page five he summarized:

... We can get a decision by merely making the judges of the election parties defendant, but if we include the State Democratic Executive Committee in the case, we feel that they will demur on the ground there is no personal liability (raising the very issue you yourself raise), as they are, in a measure, legislative officials, which will then place them before the court, asserting in their demurrer that they are an arm of the State and by virtue thereof, not subject to liability; in which case they then practically admit the resolution was passed by them ass a component part of the State organization. Even though they got away with this, we have the local judges against whom there is no question of liability.

Marshall wrote a courteous reply on March 11, obviously respecting the El Paso lawyer's position, but he summarized: "Under all the circumstances, therefore, I strongly advise that we proceed upon the beaten path pointed out by the Supreme Court of the United States in *Nixon vs Herndon.*"

Knollenberg had no choice but to file the case against the two election judges, James Condon and C. H. Kolle, but in a letter to the NAACP, advising that the suit had been filed he wrote: "The writer wants to go on record as being against the procedure; not because it is not good legally, but because I do not think it gives us what we want from practical standpoint for future use."[122]

In the months to come, he would have cause to wonder, again and again, whether or not his own position would have brought better results.

The Second Suit

The case of *Nixon v. Condon and Kolle* was filed in the United States District Court, Western District of Texas, at El Paso, on March 5, 1929. In the Plaintiff's Petition, Knollenberg was careful to trace the blame from the election judges, through the State Executive Committee, to a law of the State of Texas:

Under the instructions given them by H. O. Cregor, the Chairman of the County Democratic Executive Committee of El Paso County, Texas pursuant to the resolution of the State Executive Committee of Texas hereinafter set forth, adopted under the authority of Chapter 67 of the laws of 1927, enacted by the Legislature of the State of Texas hereinafter set forth, only white Democrats were allowed to participate in the Democratic Primary Election.

He also made clear that the whole purpose of the action by the State Legislature had been to void the effect of the decision in *Nixon v. Herndon*:

The resolution of the State Democratic Executive Committee constituted an evasion of the determination of the Supreme Court of the United States, and the 14th and 15th amendments to the Constitution of the United States, and was enacted and adopted for the purpose of denying to the plaintiff and all other negroes who belong to the Democratic party the right to vote in Democratic party primaries held in said state.

The Democratic party was the only one holding a primary in the state, and the statute was enacted for the purpose of preventing the plaintiff and other negroes of the State, who were members of the Democratic party from participating in Democratic Primary elections.

The State of Texas is a state so overwhelmingly Democratic that nomination on the Democratic ticket is equivalent to election to the office for which such Democratic candidate is nominated, and there is practically no contest for the selection of public officers within the State save that which takes place in democratic primaries.[123]

Like the first Nixon case, damages were asked in the sum of five thousand dollars, an amount which plaintiff's attorneys would not actually try to claim.

On April 3, 1929, the defendants filed a motion to dismiss the suit. They were represented by a young El Paso attorney, Ben R. Howell, then a member of the prestigious law firm of Jones, Goldstein, Hardie and Grambling. Howell later became a member of the legal staff of El Paso Natural Gas Company and in 1974 was chairman of the Texas State Board of Education.

The motion to dismiss followed in some respects the same motion in the *Nixon v. Herndon* case. It claimed that the subject matter was political in nature and that the plaintiff was not a proper party to maintain the suit. Both of these had been eloquently answered by Justice Holmes, speaking for the unanimous court. Point 3 in the motion, however, said: "There is a failure to join the necessary defendants, to wit: the members of the State Executive Committee of the Democratic Party for the State of Texas." The motion restated the question with which Justice Holmes had found it unnecessary to deal—is a primary an election?

> The primary election was not an election within the meaning of the Constitution of the United States or any laws pursuant thereto . . . but such primary election constituted merely a nomination for an election and no deprivation of any right to vote at an election is alleged in said petition.
> . . . That said petition states no cause of action against the defendants for damages for refusing a vote, for the reason that the Acts of the 40th Legislature of the State of Texas provides that the State Executive Committee of each political party shall have the right to prescribe the qualifications of its members, and that said State Executive Committee, in prescribing such qualifications, has excluded the plaintiff in this case.

Attorney Howell may have later wondered if the above assertion tied the action of the executive committee too closely to the act of the State Legislature. On May 18, he was granted leave to amend the petition and included these significant amendments:

> Irrespective of any statutory authority, the State Executive Committee of a political party has authority to determine who shall comprise its membership. . . .
> Defendants further deny that portion of plaintiff's petition which sets out that plaintiff was a Democrat, and hereby alleges that plaintiff was not a Democrat at the time plaintiff's alleged cause of action arose.[124]

United States District Judge Charles A. Boynton upheld the motion to dismiss in an opinion rendered July 31, 1929. The El Paso judge cited twenty-nine separate cases to back his decision that "The fourteenth and fifteenth amendments are each expressly and exclusively directed against action by any State." He not only held that the action prohibiting Dr. Nixon from voting was not an action by any state, but he accepted completely Howell's amended motion that it is not necessary for a political party to be authorized by the state to determine its membership.

> The Court here holds that the State Democratic Executive Committee of the State of Texas, at the time of the resolution here complained of was not a body corporate to which the Legislature of the State of Texas

could delegate authority to legislate, and that the members of the said
committee were not officials of the State of Texas . . . but only as private
individuals holding such position as members of said State Executive
Committee by virtue of action taken upon the part of members of their
respective political party; and this is also true of defendants, they acting
only as representatives of such political party.

The Court also holds that the members of a voluntary association
such as a political organization, members of the Democratic party in
Texas, possess inherent power to prescribe qualifications regulating membership of such organization or political party. That is, and was, true
without reference to the passage by the Legislature of the State of Texas
of said Article 3107, and it is not affected by passage of said Act, and
such inherent power remains and exists, just as if said Act had never
been passed.

Judge Boynton also sustained fully the contention that a primary is not an election, citing the decision in *Newberry v. United
States* (256 U.S. 232,250):

The 17th amendment, which directs that Senators be chosen by the
people, neither announced nor requires a new meaning of election, and
the word now has the same general significance as it did when the Constitution came into existence, final choice of an office by the duly qualified
electors. . . . Primaries were then unknown. Moreover, they are in no
sense elections for an office, but merely methods by which party adherents
agree upon candidates whom they intend to offer and support for ultimate
choice by all qualified electors.[125]

Again, in an El Paso District Court, issues that would affect
an entire nation were laid out clearly. Knollenberg awaited the
opportunity to get them before the Supreme Court. Nevertheless,
in a letter to Louis Marshall, he expressed his disappointment:

"We were very much disappointed in this opinion, not so
much in the decision, as we expected that, but in the reasons
therefor." In the same letter he wrote:

He also holds the primary is not an election and that the Democratic
political organization of the State of Texas is a voluntary organization,
and have the right to deprive negroes, Jews, Catholics, Methodists or
any one else that they see fit of the right to vote in the Democratic primary.

This opinion practically re-enacts into law the old Dred Scott decision
and overrules in our opinion the Slaughter House Case, the Nixon Case,
the Hopkins Case, the Child Labor Case and all that array of cases cited
by you in your excellent letter outlining your ideas in this case.

The big problem was to get the case before the Supreme Court, and citing earlier cases which the U.S. Circuit Court of Appeals had dismissed for want of jurisdiction when the controversy involved application of the Federal Constitution, Knollenberg concluded: "It is extremely desirable that this case go direct to the Supreme Court instead of through the Court of Appeals if possible."[126]

Before the week was out, he had written Marshall again, stating he had found it necessary to go to the Court of Appeals, rather than direct to the Supreme Court on a writ of error, as in the previous case. On August 9, a letter from William T. Andrews of the NAACP legal staff came to this same conclusion. Efforts were made to transfer the appeal from Circuit Court of Appeals at Fort Worth to the same Court at New Orleans, but on January 6, 1930, Knollenberg and his associates learned that the case had been set at Fort Worth for November 1930. It had been hoped that the transfer to New Orleans would move the case forward on the docket.[127] Now, in July 1930, for the fourth time, Dr. L. A. Nixon would be denied the right to vote in a Democratic Primary.

Louis Marshall possibly never read the letter of August 2, quoted above, nor the follow up letter a few weeks later. On August 2, he sailed for Europe, and in early October, during the European trip, he died. On October 24, Knollenberg was advised that Arthur B. Spingarn, long an official and legal advisor of NAACP, would take Marshall's place as chief counsel. Marshall's son James, of his father's firm, was also invited into the case.[128]

In early July 1930, before the case could be heard by the Circuit Court of Appeals, death claimed another of the NAACP's legal lights, Moorfield Storey, a long-time president of the National Association for the Advancement of Colored People. Expressing his sympathy, Fred Knollenberg asked for a picture of Storey for the president of the El Paso NAACP Chapter, Lawrence W. Washington.[129]

When the case of *Nixon v. Condon* was considered by the U.S. Circuit Court of Appeals in October 1931, attorneys were listed as Fred C. Knollenberg and E. F. Cameron of El Paso and Arthur B. Spingarn of New York as attorneys for the Appellant (Dr. Nixon) and Ben R. Howell and Thornton Hardie as attorneys for the Appellees (Condon and Kolle). The decision was handed down on

May 16, 1931, and it dealt with only one subject: "Had the State of Texas, directly or indirectly, deprived Dr. Nixon of the right to vote?"

> The Fourteenth amendment is expressly directed against prohibitions and restraints imposed by the states, and the Fifteenth protects the right to vote against denial or abridgement by any state or the United States; neither operates against private individuals or voluntary associations. A political party is a voluntary association, and as such has the inherent power to prescribe the qualifications of its members.
>
> The act of 1927 was not needed to confer such power; it merely recognized a power that already existed.[130]

The decision therefore affirmed the judgment of the District Court in El Paso. The next step would be an appeal to the Supreme Court. After several letters back and forth between Knollenberg and the NAACP attorneys, it was decided this action would be taken by means of a request for a writ of certiorari—a writ in which the Supreme Court asks for the lower courts to send up the record of a case for review. The request and supporting brief filled thirty-six pages, outlining the entire history of the case, but concentrating on the charge that the State of Texas had exercised its power to deprive Dr. Nixon of his right to vote:

> The statute declares an emergency to exist. What was the emergency in June, 1927? It was, as expressed in Section 2, the fact that on March 7, 1927, this Court had declared the existing statute restricting negro voting in Democratic primaries to be unconstitutional. That created an emergency, in that negroes might legally vote in Democratic primaries unless something were done.
>
> The respondents claimed, and the District Court and the Circuit Court of appeals held in his case, that the political parties had inherent power to determine who should vote at party primaries. The Texas legislature however, has not taken this same view. The time, place, and manner of holding Primary Elections, as well as of determining and contesting the results thereof, are comprehensively and minutely described by statutory provisions. Having already assumed control over primary elections it proceeded by Chapter 67 of the laws of 1927 to delegate to the state executive committee of every political party in the state the power to prescribe qualifications for membership and who should be qualified to vote or otherwise participate in the political parties.

Since the case was filed against the election judges, the supporting brief analyzed their position as representatives of the State of Texas:

They are clothed with the power to act in the capacity of judges at primary elections by the state itself. Though their designation may come from the party, their powers flow from the state alone and their function as judges of an election is to accomplish a state purpose. They are required to take an oath faithfully to perform their duty as officers of the election. They are empowered to keep the peace at the primary election, to enforce the anti-loitering law, to make arrests, to administer oaths and conduct examinations thereunder in order to determine the qualifications of voters.

If, therefore, these judges of election have abused their powers derived from the state and have used them as "the instrument for doing wrong," their actions are state actions.[131]

In October 1931 the Supreme Court granted the petition for a writ of certiorari and ordered the complete transcript of the case sent up to the court for review. The case was set for consideration in the October 1931 term, which would last until mid-1932. Fred Knollenberg was advised by the NAACP in December that it would not be necessary for him to go to Washington for the oral argument before the Supreme Court. The petition and the transcript of the case were the important items, and any necessary argument would be made by NAACP attorneys James Marshall and Nathan Margold.[132] There is no evidence in the correspondence contained in the Nixon papers that Knollenberg was disappointed. The file contains many cooperative letters from the El Paso attorney, and he was also permitted to file, together with his associate, E. F. Cameron, a brief on behalf of the petitioner.

Argument and Indecision

The case of *Nixon v. Condon and Kolle* was argued on January 7, 1932, with Marshall and Margold arguing for the petitioner, and Ben R. Howell for the respondents. The case was restored to the docket and reargued on March 15, and on May 2, 1932, Justice Benjamin Cardozo delivered the opinion of the five-to-four majority of the divided court. Justice Oliver Wendell Holmes, who had delivered the unanimous opinion in the *Nixon v. Herndon* case, had resigned from the court on January 11, 1932, and was replaced by Cardozo on March 14. Holmes, therefore, had heard the original argument, and Cardozo had been on the bench only one day when the case was reargued. He had been a member of the court less than two months when he delivered the majority opinion.

Cordozo's opinion starts off boldly, and the reader would be tempted to forecast a firm and sweeping decision:

> The petitioner, a Negro, has brought this action against judges of election in Texas to recover damages for their refusal by reason of his race or color to permit him to cast his vote at a primary election.
> This is not the first time that he has found it necessary to invoke the jurisdiction of the federal courts in vindication of privileges secured to him by the federal Constitution.

It is easy to find eloquent, quotable statements in the Cardozo opinion, but like many other seemingly clear documents, this one requires a careful reading of all the fine print. The associate justice seemed to ridicule the argument of the defense:

> We are told that a political party is merely a voluntary association; that it has inherent power like voluntary associations generally to determine its own membership, that the new article of the statute, adopted in place of the mandatory article of exclusion condemned by this court, has no other effect than to restore to the members of the party the power that would have been theirs if the lawmakers had been silent, and that qualifications thus established are as far aloof from the impact of constitutional restraint as those for membership in a golf club or for admission to a Masonic lodge.

The question had been effectively posed, but the justice was not about to answer it. Instead, he said simply, "Whether a political party in Texas has inherent power today without restraint by law to determine its own membership, we are not required at this time either to affirm or deny."

Cardozo then turned to the argument for the petitioner, Dr. Nixon, and it is easy to find eloquent phrases that seem to forecast a decisive conclusion:

The argument for the petitioner is that, quite apart from the article in controversy, there are other provisions of the election law whereby the privilege of unfettered choice has been withdrawn or abridged; that nomination at a primary is in many circumstances required by the statute if nomination is to be made at all; that parties and their representatives have become the custodians of official power, and that if heed is to be given to the realities of political life, they are now agencies of the State, the instruments by which government becomes a living thing.

Then, having said it so eloquently, Justice Cardozo decided it was not necessary to say it at all. Instead, he ruled:

A narrower base will serve for our judgment in the cause at hand. Whether the effect of Texas legislation has been to work so complete a transformation of the concept of a political party as a voluntary association, we do not now decide. Nothing in this opinion is to be taken as carrying with it an intimation that the court is ready or unready to follow the petitioner so far. As to that, decision must be postponed until decision becomes necessary.

In this case, the court ruled, the state had not "remitted to the party the untrammeled power to prescribe the qualifications of its members. Instead, the statute lodged the power in a committee, which excluded the petitioner and others of his race, not by virtue of any authority delegated by the party, but by virtue of an authority originating or supposed to originate in the mandate of the law."

After several pages of analysis, backed up by half a dozen or more previous cases, the decision came to "the narrower base" for the judgment of the court. The State Executive Committee was not the proper group of people to make the decision on the qualifications of the party members.

The State Executive Committee, if it is the sovereign organ of the party, is not such by virtue of any powers inherent in its being. It is, as its name imports, a committee and nothing more, a committee to be chosen by the convention, and to consist of a chairman and thirty-one members, one from each Senatorial district of the state. To this Committee, the statute here in controversy has attempted to confide authority to determine of its own motion the requisites of party membership and in so doing to speak for the party as a whole. Never has the State convention made declaration of a will to bar Negroes of the State from admission to the party ranks.

From this narrow base, the court moved nevertheless to a firm decision. Five of the nine justices agreed to the conclusion expressed by the junior member of the court:

> With the problem thus laid bare and its essentials exposed to view, the case is seen to be ruled by Nixon vs Herndon, 273 U.S. 536. Delegates of the State's power have discharged their official functions in such a way as to discriminate invidiously between white citizens and black. . . . The 14th Amendment, adopted as it was with special solicitude for the equal protection of members of the Negro race, lays a duty upon the court to level by its judgment these barriers of color.
> The judgment below is reversed and the cause remanded for further proceedings in conformity with this opinion.[133]

Back to El Paso

The case of *Nixon v. Condon*, dismissed once by the District Court at El Paso, was thus referred back to that court to be tried on the basis of the Supreme Court decision. It was October 15, 1932, and another Democratic primary election had come and gone, when judgment was finally rendered in the El Paso court:

> This cause coming on to be heard on this the 15th day of October, A. D. 1932, in open court, the plaintiff being present in person and by his attorneys, Fred C. Knollenberg and E. F. Cameron, and the defendants being present by their attorney Ben R. Howell, and a jury being waived, all matters of fact as well as of law were submitted to the court and the court having heard the pleadings read and being fully advised in the premises, doth find that the law and facts are with the plaintiff who is entitled to recover a judgment against the defendants for having been deprived of his right to vote in the Democratic Primaries; thereupon the attorneys announced in court that they had agreed that a judgment might be rendered for the amount of $1.00.
> It is, therefore, ordered adjudged and decreed that the plaintiff, L. A. Nixon, have and recover from James Condon and C. H. Kolle the sum of $1.00 and all costs in this cause incurred.[134]

It was another victory for Dr. Lawrence A. Nixon and his attorneys. Twice the highest court of the land had ruled in favor of his claim to the right to vote in a Democratic primary; but the words of the court, "government becomes a living thing," would remain an empty phrase for him and hundreds of thousands of other negroes in Texas. Another twelve years would pass by before he could walk into a Democratic primary and vote.

If the guiding forces of the Democratic party had been looking for another way to stop negroes from voting in the Democratic primaries, they needed only to read carefully the words of Justice Cardozo's opinion in *Nixon v. Condon*. While coming around to the "narrower base" that it was the State Executive Committee which lacked inherent power to decide membership qualifications of the party, the associate justice told the Democrats of Texas just exactly where that inherent power might lie. Quoting as his authority the distinguished political scientist and former British Ambassador James Bryce (*Modern Democracies*, vol. 2, p. 40), Cardozo reasoned:

Whatever inherent power a State political party has to determine the content of its membership resides in the State convention. There, platforms of principles are announced and the tests of party allegiance made known to the world. What is true in that regard of parties generally, is true more particularly in Texas, where the statute is explicit in committing to the State convention the formulation of the party faith (Article 3139).[135]

The Democratic party of Texas was alert to the implied invitation, and less than a month after the Supreme Court decision, the State Democratic Convention passed a resolution, dated May 24, 1932: "Be it resolved that all white citizens of the State of Texas who are qualified to vote under the constitution and laws of the State shall be eligible to membership in the Democratic party, and as such, to participate in its deliberations."[136]

It was easy to be cynical about the prospects for the negro to vote in Texas Democratic primaries, and one such reaction came from a young Texan, William N. Stokes, Jr., a law student at Yale University. In April 1932, he wrote Fred Knollenberg asking for information on the forthcoming *Nixon v. Condon* decision and commenting: "I had some correspondence with you several years ago with relation to your part in the *Nixon vs Herndon* case. At that time I was an undergraduate college student with legal inclinations."

On May 7, after the Supreme Court decision, he wrote Knollenberg his congratulations "upon your victory" but continued:

I have wondered all along as to the ultimate wisdom of such actions, but certainly one could have no quarrel with the legal manner in which they have been handled. My doubts as to whether or not the actions are wise is based upon my belief that anything the Supreme Court, the Bible, or the President of the United States may say will be futile to give the negro his right so long as the widespread desire remains to keep him from exercising them. I have thought that it would be as difficult to cram the negro voter down the throat of the South as it is to cram prohibition down the throat of the New England yankee or the New York bowery bum. I know that in some parts of Texas, if every legal recourse is exhausted, the result will be obtained by return to "Clucker" methods. Thank heaven that isn't true in my own section, where I don't think many of the people care a great deal one way or the other. The idea seems to work itself out of Cardozo's opinion. I have wondered if the talk about the conventions wasn't as complete a surprise to you as it was to me? And I have also wondered as to his real reasons for using it at all. I was frankly disappointed in the opinion, because in the first place it seemed to make too many apologies, and in the second place, he could have clinched his whole logical argument without mentioning the party convention and its authority at all. . . .

I am certain that after this opinion, the convention when it meets on May 24th will delegate the same power to the executive committee, and then you will have five more years of no negro suffrage on your hands, and the Supreme Court will find itself compelled either to take another long hurdle, or to refuse to jump altogether.

The Yale law student was a good prophet, but if Fred Knollenberg shared his pessimism, it was not reflected in his actions. On October 22, 1932, following the final action in the El Paso District Court, James Marshall wrote to Knollenberg: "I think the result is highly satisfactory, and congratulate you upon the splendid work which you have contributed to it." A week later, October 29, Walter White wrote the El Paso attorney that his proposal for a third suit was under consideration by the legal committee, and on January 4, 1933, White wrote: "May I tell you how very grateful we are for your willingness to share with us the present situation by agreeing to handle this third case at the stipulated figure."[137]

There is nothing in the Nixon papers, however, to indicate that negotiations proceeded further. Certainly no third case was filed from El Paso, although Dr. L. A. Nixon was ready in case the NAACP needed him. Mrs. Nixon recalls that, through the years, he faithfully paid his poll tax and presented himself at the polls on primary election days. Newspapers and radio stations began calling him at Democratic primary time to ask if he were going to vote, and he would answer quietly but firmly, "I'm going to try."

Other Attempts to Press the Cause

Perhaps the NAACP felt it was best to attack from some new areas. Now that the Nixon cases had broken down some of the barriers, there was activity in many parts of the country to bring more cases into court for new judgments. Justice Cardozo's words, "decision must be postponed until decision becomes necessary," left a judicial door open for such attempts. In Virginia, a Federal District Court had, for the first time, acknowledged that a primary is an election, and this decision was upheld by the Court of Appeals. The case differed from the Nixon cases only in the fact that the State of Virginia paid for its primary elections, while in Texas the candidates were required to pay the cost of primaries. It was an important difference, but one more step along the negro's tortuous path to complete enfranchisement.[138]

In Houston, Texas, a negro law firm, Atkins, Wesley and Nabrit, was looking for an opportunity to bring a case before the federal court. With the help of NAACP, the three partners had succeeded in filing a separate brief in the *Nixon v. Condon* case. They had had considerable correspondence with Fred Knollenberg in the case and exchanged opinions as to the course the argument should take.[139] Then, in 1934, the Houston firm found an opportunity to file a case of its own.

Grovey v. Townsend

In July 1934, ten years after Dr. Nixon challenged the Texas statute that forbade negroes to vote in Democratic primaries, R. R. Grovey entered the office of Albert Townsend, county clerk in Houston, and requested an absentee ballot to vote in the forthcoming Democratic primary. His request was denied on the basis that the Democratic Convention of Texas had limited membership in the party to "white citizens of the state of Texas." Atkins, Wesley and Nabrit felt that a new element in this case might be

introduced to the Supreme Court: a county clerk is an elected
official of the state of Texas and not an official of the Democratic
party, and since the Federal Court in Virginia had found that a
primary is an election, County Clerk Townsend appeared to have
violated the fourteenth and fifteenth amendments by denying
Grovey the absentee ballot.

The case was handled in an unusual manner. Instead of filing
in Houston Federal Court, the attorneys took it before a justice
of the peace, in Houston's Precinct One, asking for ten dollars
damages to Grovey for his loss of the voting privilege. Then, in
what must be considered a bold move, Grovey's lawyers asked the
Supreme Court for a writ of certiorari from Justice Court, Precinct
One. Strictly speaking, a justice court is not a court of record in
Texas, so it would have been necessary for attorneys to have a
transcript made of the proceedings and have them properly certified
and made ready for submission to the Supreme Court for review.

The seeming audacity of the move may have caught the atten-
tion of the nation's highest tribunal. In any event, the petition was
granted; the court agreed to review the transcript, direct from a
Texas justice of the peace to the Supreme Court of the United
States, with no intermediate steps in the Federal district or appeals
courts, and on March 11, 1935, *Grovey v. Townsend* was argued
before the court. While the NAACP is known to have evidenced
a strong interest in the case and probably consulted extensively
with the Houston attorneys, none of the distinguished New York,
Boston and Washington lawyers so active in the two Nixon cases
are listed in *Grovey v. Townsend*. The only lawyer appearing for
the petitioner was J. Alston Atkins of Houston. Argument lasted
but one day, and the case was taken under advisement.

Those who had so hopefully pursued the case could not help
noting that the decision was rendered on April Fool's Day, April
1, 1935. Justice Owen J. Roberts wrote the opinion of a unanimous
court, and he found that, even in this case, the action against the
aspiring negro voter was not state action: "Here the qualifications
of citizens to participate in party councils and to vote in party
primaries have been declared by the representatives of the party
in convention assembled, and this action upon its face is not state
action."

The fact that it was a county clerk and not the party's election
judges who turned down Grovey's request made no difference,

and Justice Roberts decreed: "We find no ground for holding that the respondent has, in obedience to the mandate of the law of Texas, discriminated against the petitioner, or denied him any right guaranteed by the Fourteenth and Fifteenth Amendments." The judgment of the Houston justice court was affirmed.[140]

Grovey v. Townsend was a low point in the negro's struggle for effective suffrage. It appeared the court would continue to maintain that membership in the political parties could be determined by the state conventions, conventions in which, in many of the states, negroes could not have any part. Those who supported the right of black people to vote in primary elections could only look at the changing face of the Supreme Court.

In May 1935, only a month after the Grovey decision, the Supreme Court struck down one of the keystone New Deal reforms, the National Industrial Recovery Act, finding it unconstitutional. The following January, it invalidated the Agricultural Adjustment Act. President Roosevelt tried to influence the court by his public statements on the issues, and when that failed he tried sterner measures. In February 1937, he suggested to Congress that it authorize him to appoint one additional justice for every man on the Supreme Court over seventy years of age. There were seven of these septuagenarians on the court, and the proposal brought nationwide controversy. Roosevelt failed in his attempt to "pack the court," but time and fate solved the problem. By the time the fall term of the court came around in 1943, seven of the nine justices who had united in the *Grovey v. Townsend* decision had died or resigned. Only Owen J. Roberts, who had written the decision, and Harlan F. Stone, who had become chief justice, remained. Roosevelt had appointed seven new justices to give the court a strong liberal cast.[141]

Smith v. Allwright

With this dramatic change in the high court, it was obviously time to try again on the subject of negro voting rights. Again the site was Houston, and the nature of the case was similar to that of the two Nixon cases. On June 27, 1940, Lonnie Smith, whose poll tax receipt listed his color as "black," presented himself at Harris County Precinct 48 and attempted to vote in the Democratic primary. When he was refused, as he knew he would be, his lawyers, including Atkins, Wesley and Nabrit, took their complaint to the Federal District Court in Houston, asking damages from the election judges, S. E. Ellwright and James E. Liuzza. When the *Smith v. Allwright* complaint was dismissed by the District Court, an appeal was taken to the U.S. Circuit Court of Appeals for the Fifth District.[142]

When the appeal was made, the legal heavy artillery began to move into place. The chief counsel for Lonnie Smith before the Court of Appeals was Thurgood Marshall, then chief legal officer for the NAACP. But thirty-three years old, he had graduated eight years earlier at the head of his class at Howard University Law School, and began a brilliant legal career that brought him to the NAACP's national legal staff at age twenty-eight. In 1967, he would be appointed by President Lyndon B. Johnson as the first negro ever named to the United States Supreme Court.[143]

Marshall probably expected to lose the argument before the Court of Appeals. His chief purpose was to get the case before a new and vastly changed United States Supreme Court. His request for a writ of certiorari was granted and the case went to the high court for review. Argument was set for November 10, 1943, and in this case the NAACP had an abundance of help. Joining Thurgood Marshall in the argument before the Supreme Court was another brilliant young negro lawyer, William H. Hastie, the thirty-nine-year-old dean of the Howard University Law School in Washington, D. C. Hastie had served as assistant solicitor of the Department of the Interior and as judge of the United States District Court in the Virgin Islands. Later he would serve as governor of the Virgin Islands, and a twenty-two-year career as judge of the United States Court of Appeals.[144]

The Democratic Party and the State of Texas, too, were represented by an array of legal talent, George W. Barcus of Austin for the party and the accused precinct judges, and Attorney General Gerald Mann for the State of Texas. Wright Morrow, Democratic national committeeman for the State of Texas, also filed a brief for the party. Briefs in behalf of the petitioner were filed by Arthur Garfield Hays for the American Civil Liberties Union, and by attorneys for the Committee on Constitutional Liberties, the National Lawyers Guild, and the Workers Defense League. The argument lasted for two days, November 10 and 12, 1943, and then was called back for reargument on January 12, 1944. The decision was announced on April 3.

No announcement was made as to the lineup of the judges on either side, but the opinion was delivered by one of the Roosevelt appointees, Associate Justice Stanley Reed. Justice Felix Frankfurter, also appointed by Franklin D. Roosevelt, announced that he concurred in the opinion. The only dissenting opinion announced was that of Associate Justice Owen T. Roberts, who had written the opinion in the *Grovey v. Townsend* case. Roberts defended the previous position of the court and complained of the many recent cases in which the court had reversed itself. Reed defended the court majority with the words "When convinced of a former error, this court has never felt constrained to follow precedent."[145]

That the court had, through its majority, done an about face on some of its previous holdings was evident from the uncompromising words of Justice Reed:

> Primary elections are conducted by the party under state statutory authority. . . . We think that this statutory system for the selection of party nominees for inclusion on the general election ballot makes the party which is required to follow these legislative directions an agency of the state.
>
> The United States is a constitutional democracy. Its organic law grants to all citizens a right to participate in the choice of elected officials without restriction by any state because of race. This grant to the people of the opportunity for choice is not to be nullified by a state through casting its electoral process in a form which permits a private organization to practice racial discrimination in the election. Constitutional rights would be of little value if they could be thus indirectly denied. . . .
>
> Here we are applying, contrary to the recent decision in Grovey vs Townsend, the well established principle of the Fifteenth Amendment, forbidding the abridgement by a state of a citizen's right to vote. Grovey vs Townsend is overruled, judgment reversed.[146]

Justice Reed had not hesitated to take those steps which Holmes and Cardozo had found it unnecessary to take, or to reject the position taken by Roberts for the entire court in the *Grovey v. Townsend* case. The position of the court was now clear: A primary is an election under the meaning of the fifteenth amendment; and even if a political party is considered a private organization, it is an agency of the state in its conduct of primary elections which determine what candidates go on the final election ballot.

Government Becomes a Living Thing

The decision was not announced until long after the January 31 deadline for paying the Texas poll tax and becoming a registered voter for both primary and general elections. Nevertheless, in El Paso, where the battle for negro voting in Democratic primaries had begun twenty years earlier, 290 negroes had paid their $1.75 poll tax for the year 1944.[147] On July 20, the Democratic chairman of El Paso sent official notices to judges of all voting precincts, calling attention to the Supreme Court decision and instructing them to permit properly registered negroes to vote in the Democratic Primary of July 22. The Negro Voters League of El Paso called a meeting for the night of July 20 in Mount Zion Baptist Church. The league chairman was Le Roy White, the man who had left Cameron, Texas, thirty-four years earlier, in a boxcar with Dr. Lawrence A. Nixon, to make a new home in El Paso.[148]

In Houston's Precinct 48, Lonnie Smith was the first person in line to vote in the Democratic Primary. In Precinct 28 of that city, negroes controlled the precinct convention held immediately after the polls closed. They elected a white delegate to the Harris County Democratic Convention.[149]

In all their reports of negro participation in the Democratic primary, El Paso newspapers did not mention that the battle for this participation had started in El Paso, twenty years earlier. None of the stories mentioned Dr. Nixon, but the *Herald-Post* reported on July 19: "For the first time in the history of El Paso County, negroes will be allowed to vote in Saturday's Democratic Primary." The basis of *Nixon v. Herndon* had been that the petitioner was an active Democrat who had voted regularly in the primaries until he was excluded by an act of the Texas State Legislature in 1923.

Years later, in a letter to Walter White, executive secretary of the NAACP, Dr. Nixon wrote:

In 1910, I came to El Paso. I had been out of Meharry four years. At that time, we were voting in the Democratic primary. I voted in every election up to 1924. Candidates sought our votes, and those of us who thought it was our duty to vote had no other choice but to vote with the Democrats. The Democratic primary has always been *the* election in Texas. Many people here do not bother to go to the polls in the general election. Republicanism exists in Texas, many of us think, only to control patronage when the party is in power in the nation. It was natural that we should fight the vicious, conceited, suicidal measure hatched by the 1924 [1923] Texas Legislature., We had here a branch of the NAACP. The negro in El Paso, as in all other localities, means to fight always to preserve the Constitution of the United States and to make democracy a fact in this land, and not a lying cloak to hide behind. There were some, of course, who thought as my father did back in the years: that a negro should not want to vote with the Democrats. A few were apathetic and a number had that fear that always makes impotent a large number of Americans, leaving actual control of affairs, local and national, in the hands of a few.[150]

On July 22, 1944, it had been twenty years, lacking a few days, since he had first been turned away from an El Paso Democratic primary. Fittingly, a welcome rainstorm broke a long El Paso drought, and Dr. and Mrs. Lawrence A. Nixon walked to the polling place, presented their poll tax receipts, and voted.

So Excellent a Person

In the fall of 1931, as the *Nixon v. Condon* case was being set for its Supreme Court hearing, the NAACP chapter in Houston began taking a strong interest in the case, and as noted earlier, a Houston negro law firm filed a brief in support of Dr. Nixon. On November 2, Walter White, national secretary of the organization, wrote to E. O. Smith, president of the Houston chapter, explaining the circumstances of the two Nixon cases. The letter contains this sentence: "Dr. Nixon was so excellent a person on whom to base this contest that we decided to prepare, file, and fight his case as a test of the validity of the enabling act, and we have handled it from its inception.[151]

After the first Nixon case, there was no doubt among the attorneys in New York and in El Paso that, of all the negroes in Texas, Dr. Nixon was the man to be the plaintiff in the second case. In a letter to attorney Arthur B. Spingarn, in September 1928, Fred Knollenberg had written: "It seems to us that the psychological effect upon the Supreme Court in using Dr. Nixon would be of immense benefit in the case."[152]

Dr. Nixon Takes a Bride

He was the right man in the right place. More than that, he was a good man—an admirable man. So he seemed to Drusilla Tandy Porter, when she came to El Paso in October 1929. Divorced from her first husband, Knoxville newspaper editor Webster L. Porter, she had returned with her daughter Dorothy to live with her parents in Toledo, Ohio. There, in 1929, she suffered a severe attack of asthma, and was advised by her physician to move to a warm, dry climate, suggesting the area of El Paso, Tucson and Phoenix. She knew no one at all in the area, and to a negro woman in 1929, this presented many problems. You couldn't just go to a hotel while you awaited suitable housing, for most hotels would not take negro guests. You had to know where you could eat. It helped a great deal to know someone.

Drusilla's sister, Edna Tandy, had a suggestion. Edna had a strong interest in politics and was an active member of the National Association for the Advancement of Colored People. Earlier that same year she had attended a convention of the NAACP in Denver. There she had met a fine gentleman from El Paso, a colored physician who had recently taken his case to the Supreme Court to secure for negroes the right to vote in Democratic primaries. Perhaps if Drusilla would write him, he could be helpful.

With the introduction from her sister, Drusilla wrote her first letter to Dr. Lawrence A. Nixon, asking if he could help her find a place to stay in El Paso while she underwent treatment for her asthma. Within a surprisingly short time she had an answer. One of his patients, a widow, lived at 411 Tornillo Street, and would be glad to have Mrs. Porter stay at her house.

El Paso did not present an inviting appearance on this first visit. It was later October and the first cold blast of winter was moving in—wind, cold, dust, and just enough snow to add to the discomfort without adding a mantle of beauty. To the visitor from Toledo, where she was accustomed to two- and three-story houses, much of the town had a squat appearance, and the little house on Tornillo Street seemed hardly more than a shack. But her host was hospitable, and Dr. Nixon was kind and generous in helping her find her way about in a community which was more western than southern, but which still clung stubbornly to the laws and traditions of racial segregation. Medically, Dr. Nixon became her physician, and by February, the patient felt well enough to travel. She left for Tucson, and from there returned to her home in Toledo, probably without serious thought of returning again to El Paso.

She had some correspondence with Dr. Nixon during the next few years. She knew about the success of his second Supreme Court case, and she knew he was a widower, but any deeper interest, if it existed, was dormant. Then, about 1933, Drusilla was taking a trip to California by train. The train would be stopping in El Paso at midnight, and she thought it would be pleasant to see some of her friends. From Kansas City, she sent a telegram to Dr. Nixon, asking if someone might come down to the station to meet her. The doctor himself came, and in the first gesture of something beyond friendship and the doctor-patient relationship, he brought her a box of candy and his picture. The letters became more frequent between them, and more personal, and when she returned to El Paso again, in 1935, she soon became Mrs. Lawrence A. Nixon.

The wedding took place in Las Cruces, November 14, 1935, and Mrs. Nixon laughingly recalls, "I guess we were eloping!" Dr. Nixon's friend, the Rev. Le Roy White, assistant pastor of the Shiloh Baptist Church, performed the ceremony, nearly twenty-five years after his journey to El Paso from Cameron in a boxcar.

Mrs. Nixon has many happy memories of their first home in El Paso, a combination home and office, with a pleasant Japanese garden, located at 2029 Myrtle Avenue. Adjoining the home was the Myrtle Avenue Methodist Church. Dr. Nixon was one of its organizers and trustees and a faithful member of its choir, and the new Mrs. Nixon, too, became an active and valuable member.

There were other memories not so pleasant. The streetcar into town ran right down Myrtle Avenue, but Drusilla Nixon could never bring herself to ride it. Her complexion is lighter than that of many white women, and there might be questions as to why she was sitting in the rear of the car, in the section marked "colored." She was proud of her race, proud of her husband, and when she found it necessary to go to town, and he was unable to take her in their car, she simply walked.[153]

Other Breakthroughs Followed

More than three years had passed since the questionable victory in the *Nixon v. Condon* case, and another nine years would go by before the *Smith v. Allwright* decision made it possible for the Nixons to vote in Democratic primaries. President Lyndon B. Johnson, in recalling the legislative struggle for equal voting rights, has written: "Once the black man's voice could be translated into ballots, many other breakthroughs would follow, and they would follow as a consequence of the black man's legitimate power as an American citizen, and not as a gift of the white man."[154]

In El Paso, certainly, the breakthroughs began to come, and the doors began to open in the years that followed the black voter's accession to complete voting privileges. Dr. Nixon began to notice that some of the people who had stopped speaking to him during the long years of the Supreme Court cases had become cordial again. Some of the doors opened easily; others were subjects of controversy.

The "colored" sections of streetcars and buses were eliminated with little fanfare. The end of segregation in the schools was a more difficult problem. In May 1954, Thelma White graduated from Douglass High School in El Paso, the valedictorian of her class. That fall, she applied for admission to Texas Western College (now the University of Texas at El Paso), and was refused because of her race. J. M. Whitaker, superintendent of the El Paso Independent School District at this writing, was then registrar of Texas Western. He recalls that he informed Miss White he was carrying out the orders of the Board of Regents of the University of Texas in denying admission to any negro students. She enrolled that year in New Mexico A and M College (now New Mexico State University) in Las Cruces. In April 1955, she and her parents filed suit in Federal Court for admission to Texas Western.

School Segregation Ends

The case came to trial in July 1955, and by that time school segregation in El Paso was on its way out. On June 21, 1955, the Board of Trustees of the El Paso Independent School District passed a resolution stating simply that segregation of the races would no longer be enforced in public schools of the district.[155] El Paso was the first major school district in Texas to adopt such a resolution. Other school districts of the area had begun to take similar action when Thelma White's case came to trial. By July 18, the day of the decision, Texas Western College officials were ready to admit Miss White, and appeared in court to testify to that effect. Lawyers for the National Association for the Advancement of Colored People, however, were not satisfied with this offer, but insisted upon a court judgment. Thurgood Marshall and Robert L. Carter were listed among the attorneys for the petitioner, and an eloquent black attorney from Dallas, U. Simpson Tate, made the argument before the court. A record had to be made, he insisted, and the court issued a judgment that Thelma White was entitled to admission to Texas Western College of the University of Texas.[156]

The Nixon family welcomed this decision, for they were deeply devoted to education. Dr. Nixon's son, Lawrence Joseph Nixon, was educated at the University of California, and for more than forty years he has been an outstanding newspaperman in Pittsburgh, Pennsylvania. Mrs. Nixon's oldest daughter, Dorothy, became in every respect a member of the Nixon family. Dorothy Nixon graduated with honors from Douglass High School in El Paso, and then attended Talledaga College, a denominational school in Alabama. She next secured a Master's degree from the Yale University school of nursing and returned to El Paso to become one of the outstanding nurses at both Providence Hospital and Hotel Dieu. In 1969, District 1 of the Texas Nurses Association named her Nurse of the Year.

Edna, the first daughter of the Nixon marriage, was one of the first black students at El Paso's Loretto Academy, where she graduated with honors. By that time, Texas Western College was open to students of all races. Edna was an outstanding student there, was listed in *Who's Who of American Colleges and Universities*, and was honored at homecoming as an outstanding member of the college band. She married Dr. W. J. McIver a few days after he received his medical degree in 1962 from Dr. Nixon's alma mater, Meharry College of Nashville. Dr. Nixon attended the graduation ceremonies on the fifty-sixth anniversary of his own graduation. Dr. McIver served for five years at William Beaumont General Hospital in El Paso, one year in Viet Nam, and three years in Germany before moving to Albuquerque, where he is a prominent surgeon.

A third Nixon daughter, Ann, suffers a handicap and is under the tender care of her mother at their home in El Paso.

Dorothy married Myron Davis, skilled in various building trades, and together they established the La Luz Motel on Highway 80 leading into El Paso. For many years it was a haven of refuge for travelers of all races on the busy east-west highway, the only quality motel in El Paso open to black travelers, and billboards along the highway proclaimed its open policy.

Commercial Segregation Ends

It was not until the early 1960s that negroes could claim access to other first class hotels and motels in El Paso. Nor were they admitted to many of the first class restaurants. As for places of entertainment, most downtown and suburban theatres turned black patrons away, and even some of the drive-ins refused them admission. A black patron had to find out which would accept him and which would not. There was a widely circulated story of a black woman who telephoned a drive-in theatre to ask if she might be admitted to the picture "I Passed for White." She was given the answer "not unless you can pass for white."

In June 1962, the City Council of the City of El Paso drew up and passed a public accommodations ordinance. Its most important section said:

> It shall be unlawful for any person, firm, association, or corporation, or any agent, servant, or employee thereof in the City of El Paso, to refuse, deny, or withhold from any person for any reason, directly or indirectly, relating to the race, color, ethnic background, or national origin of such person, any of the accommodations, advantages, facilities, or services offered to the general public by places of public accommodation.[157]

Mayor Ralph Seitsinger vetoed the ordinance, stating that the same results could be achieved, and were rapidly being achieved by voluntary means, without applying the force of law. The City Council unanimously overrode his veto, with Alderman Ted Bender flying back from a California vacation to help cast the overriding vote. The onrush of disputes and recriminations which the mayor feared did not materialize and El Paso citizens generally accepted the new open accommodations policy.

It was not until December 1969, that the City of El Paso adopted an ordinance providing open access for all races to the purchase and rental of housing.[158] This decision was unanimous, as the ordinance was necessary in order for Mayor Peter de Wetter and his council to obtain major federal grants for public housing.

Sixteen years before the open housing ordinance passed, Dr. Lawrence A. Nixon and his family decided to move into a larger and better home. In 1952, they purchased a lot and began building a home at 426 Pendale Road. They would be the first negro family in the area, a rural section that was fast becoming residential. Mrs. Nixon recalls that, just as they were about to move in, she received a telephone call inquiring if this was the Mrs. Nixon who would be moving to Pendale Road. "Oh, oh!" Mrs. Nixon thought, "Here it comes." The voice on the other end of the telephone identified herself, "This is Mrs. Fred Ward, and you're going to be our neighbors. I just want to welcome you and tell you how anxious we are to get acquainted."

Captain Fred Ward and his wife, Frederica (Freddie) were the right people to make the Nixons welcome. They were widely traveled, and had spent some years in Washington, D. C., where Mrs. Ward was employed at the Pan American Union. Here and elsewhere, they became close friends with people of many nations and many races. One of Freddie's favorite quotations was, "We are all fellow passengers on the planet earth." The Wards looked back upon their acquaintance with the Nixon family with gratitude and enthusiasm. Freddie's enthusiasm grew as she talked:

> Drusilla and her husband had charm; they were cultivated—so calm—gracious and handsome people. I would call them the best that man can be as a human being. Their home became a spacious hacienda, with well kept pecan grove and lovely gardens. Drusilla could touch anything and make it grow. We were often at their home and they at ours. They were well read and intellectual. They entertained graciously, and we had the opportunity of meeting so many interesting people who were their guests. They are among our very dearest friends.

Both Mrs. Ward and Mrs. Nixon recalled with pleasure the actions of the Wards in joining in the activities of the Ambassador's Club, an organizationl largely composed of members of the El

Paso black community. But Fred and Freddie were happy to participate and delighted with their interesting new associates. Within a few years, the Nixons purchased some investment property at North Loop and Zaragosa Roads and moved from the Pendale Road home, but their association with the Wards continued and they gained many more new friends in the lower valley.[159]

Medical Society Admission Granted

Many other doors were opening for the Nixon family. In 1955, it became possible for Dr. Nixon to be admitted to the Texas State Medical Association and the El Paso County Medical Society. The question of deleting the word "white" from the state association's constitution had come before the House of Delegates at its 1952 convention and the proposal was tabled. In 1955, at the TMA Convention in Fort Worth, the proposal appeared headed for a similar fate after Dr. J. M. Travis, of Jacksonville, Texas, gave a summary of reports from other medical associations throughout the South, all intended to support his expressed position, "I feel that the negro has been well treated and has made unbelievable progress in our civilization, and I feel that he fills a very important place in our community. This does not imply that we should give him equal social rights in our homes and private institutions, and this is what we are asking to be done. . . . I oppose changing the Constitution."

After Dr. Travis' statement, Dr. J. Leighton Green of El Paso took the floor. Dr. Green recalled that this was the only speech he made during the years he served as a member of the House of delegates. His words are here quoted with Dr. Green's permission:

I would like to preface my few remarks by saying that my great-grandfather owned slaves in South Carolina. Both of my grandfathers served in the Army of the Confederacy. I was born and reared and educated in the South. I am not a "damyankee." I think I know and understand Negroes.

I believe every man here would like to do the best thing for the profession of medicine in Texas. The trouble is that we do not always see exactly together on what is best for the profession. I feel that deleting the word "white" from our Constitution would be a step forward for the Texas Medical Association. I am going to tell you why. In the first place, I think it is the right thing to do. Our country has been criticized throughout the world because we profess to give equal rights to everybody and we don't give equal rights to the man with the colored skin.

Have you ever been in a foreign country and tried to convince an educated national of that country that the American attitude toward the negro was right? Well, I have, and I have found it to be the most indefensible of all things American. Have you ever tried to convince a 12- or 14-year-old boy why a respectable and educated man could not get a decent hotel room because he had a black skin? You will find it pretty difficult.

We are not going to tell the El Paso County Medical Society to admit Negroes to that society. Be deleting the word "white" we simply give the society the privilege of admitting these doctors if the members see fit. It would still be on individual personality and qualifications.

The second reason I think we should delete this word is to bring better medical service to certain segments of our population, because association with white doctors would stimulate these colored doctors to stay up to date and would make better doctors out of them. It would stimulate their pride. They would attend staff meetings, state medical meetings, and national meetings, and it would make better doctors out of them.

In the third place, it would improve our interracial relations. I think the communists would hate it. Our attitude toward the Negro has been the best ammunition for the propaganda of the communists. I think this would be one way to spike their guns.

In the fourth place, I think it is expedient. We waited until the Supreme Court has already ruled that segregation is unconstitutional. Are we going to wait until some federal law says we have to admit negro doctors to all our public hospitals? I personally would prefer to take the initiative and do something on our own before it is shoved down our throats.

In the fifth place, it would reflect credit upon our profession. This would convince the world we are interested in giving good medical care to all classes of people. I do not believe that social equality is a great problem.

To summarize, I think it is the right thing to do, it would improve medical care to certain people, it would improve interracial relations, it is expedient, and it would reflect credit upon the medical profession.

There followed speeches against deleting the word "white," given by doctors from Marshall, Corpus Christi, and Fort Worth, but Dr. Green had evidently turned the tide. Dr. John L. Matthews, of San Antonio, pointed out that his society had deleted the word "white" three years previous and had been reminded that it was out of harmony with the state association. Nevertheless, the Bexar County Medical Society had voted not to restore the word "white" to its constitution. Then, by voice vote the House of Delegates voted against returning the proposal to committee. Individual ballots were passed out, and the doctors voted 102 to 32 to delete the word "white" from the membership requirements in the constitution.[160]

In El Paso, medical friends of Dr. Nixon informed him he was eligible to join the Medical Society. He thanked them, but believed he was drawing too near to his retirement, and Medical Society records show he never again applied.

The Myrtle Avenue Methodist Church became more and more involved with inter-church activities with other congregations and other denominations. In 1972, with members of the black community having moved to many areas of El Paso and joined many congregations, the Myrtle Avenue Church was no longer conveniently located. Its members joined with another Methodist group, largely whites, to form the St. James Methodist Church on Lomaland Drive. But Dr. Nixon was not present to see these fruits of his pioneering efforts in behalf of his church.

Death of Dr. Lawrence A. Nixon

In late February 1966, Dr. and Mrs. Nixon suffered injuries in an automobile accident. Complications following the injuries brought about the death of the eighty-two-year-old physician on March 6. The funeral was a rich outpouring of respect and friendship by people of varied races and backgrounds. Among the pallbearers was Captain Fred Ward.

Some measure of the high respect Dr. Nixon enjoyed among people of his own race in El Paso can be found in a tribute paid him on February 4, 1968, in a special memorial service commemorating Negro History Week. Mrs. Johnny Calvert, one of the veteran teachers at Douglass School, the now integrated school which had served negro children long and well, gave this appraisal of his life and work:

> For his beautiful life we pay tribute to this man who was not born great, nor did he have greatness thrust upon him. He achieved greatness! Not through his profession, but through honorable conduct and a noble disposition.

Dr. L. A. Nixon was one of the most humble men I have ever known. In his unassuming manner, his conversations, which were never punctuated with the personal pronoun "I," he always made one feel that he was genuinely interested in you and your activities. Never from meeting him and talking with him would one suspect that he was famous. Yet famous indeed he was, because his name is familiar to every student of Constitutional history. It was Dr. Nixon who challenged a law enacted by the Texas legislature denying negroes the right to vote in primary elections.

Dr. Nixon was a philosopher—making any conversation with him a delight. He had a deep abiding faith in people. Surely his name is written in the book as one who loved his fellow men.

He was a gentle man, possessing all the qualities that we associate with the word gentleman. No one who knew him can conceive of his ever displaying rudeness in any form.

His soft voice, impeccable manners, sincerity, dedication as a family man, kindness and cheerful disposition were attributes which caused all who knew him to respect him.

Dr. Nixon was a philanthropist. He gave freely of his possessions for worthwhile causes. Myrtle Avenue Methodist Church records show that, as a Trustee, he was responsible for saving the Church from financial disaster on more than one occasion. He was a life member of the NAACP. He gave service and finance to organizations he thought would improve our community.

It is indeed proper that we pay tribute to so great a citizen, who left his mark so vividly in the minds and hearts of all of us. We are proud that the City of El Paso recognized his contributions by naming a street in his honor.[161]

His life is a challenge to each of us, a life to emulate. In attempting to adequately pay tribute to Dr. L. A. Nixon, I found the words of George Bernard Shaw strikingly appropriate for Dr. Nixon's philosophy of life: "Life is no brief candle for me. It is a sort of splendid torch which I have got hold of for the moment, and I want to make it burn as brightly as possible before handing it on to future generations."[162]

Along with Dr. Nixon's mild and cultured manner there went a firm devotion to principle. This was reflected in his letter to NAACP Secretary Walter White, quoted earlier:

Black men have learned from their experience on the American continent that the things we want we must fight for, using peace and perseverance. We know the futility of riot and murder. We will never ally ourselves with enemies of our country. We will continue to fight for the Constitution of the United States. We will never sanction discrimination against ourselves or any other people.[163]

His Widow Sees the Progress

Mrs. Nixon was able to accept the death of her husband with serenity and an adjustment to a lonelier life which was nevertheless busy and productive. She was active in church organizations, gardening, and the care of her daughter. She also found time to do research and writing on the story of Estebanico, the Moorish slave who accompanied Alvar Nunez Cabeza de Vaca and the first European visitors to the area of El Paso.

But life held more sorrow for her. On August 19, 1970, Dorothy Nixon Davis, her husband Myron and their three children, with Mrs. Nixon's brother, his daughter and her two sons, were traveling in a camper on the freeway near Palm Springs, California. Suddenly, unexplainably, the automobile exploded and burst into flames. Of the nine persons in the car, there was but one survivor, the son of Dorothy and Myron Davis. He was taken into the family of Edna and her husband Dr. W. J. McIver, in Albuquerque.

Mrs. Nixon has found the strength to accept life with courage and dignity. Quoting the words of Job, "The Lord gave and the Lord hath taken away," she reasoned, "Life is a blending of joy and sorrow, and we must learn to accept them as they come and to find that, in the balance, there is more joy than sorrow." She rejoices in her daughters, in her grandchildren, and in the many opportunities to all of them, which would not have been available a few short years ago. She sees finer homes, better employment, better education, and better community acceptance for her people. She reflects with quiet pride that these doors were opened, in large measure, as a result of that first door of equal opportunity at the ballot box, opened for a quiet, sincere and dedicated man who was in the right place at the right time, Dr. Lawrence A. Nixon of El Paso.

REFERENCES

1 Copy, Mrs. L. A. Nixon, El Paso, Texas.
2 *El Paso Times*, April 18, 1924 (R. M. Dudley Scrapbooks, Archives, El Paso Public Library).
3 Lawrence D. Rice, *The Negro in Texas* (Baton Rouge: Louisiana State University Press, 1971), 35.
4 Robert C. Colner, *James Stephen Hogg* (Austin: University of Texas Press, 1959), 278.
5 Maude Cuney Hare, *Norris Wright Cuney, A Tribune of the Black People* (New York: Crisis Publishing Co., 1913), 21.
6 Rice, 21.
7 Rice, 79.
8 Rice, 100-111.
9 Rice, 127.
10 Rice, 44-45.
11 Ira T. Taylor, *The Cavalcade of Jackson County* (San Antonio: Naylor Co. 1938), 305.
12 Rice, 89-90.
13 *Marshall Tri-Weekly Herald*, October 11, 1876.
14 *Marshall Tri-Weekly Herald*, November 4, 5, 9, 1886.
15 United States Senate, *Testimony on the Alleged Election Outrages in Texas,* Senate Miscellaneous Documents 62, 50th Cong., 2d sess., 1889.
16 Rice, 120.
17 *Terry v. Adams,* 545 U.S. 461 (1953); summarized in James Morton Smith and Paul L. Murphy, *Liberty and Justice* (New York: Alfred A. Knopf, 1958), 555-57.
18 A. J. Sowell, *History of Fort Bend County* (Waco: W. M. Morrison, 1964), 327-31.
19 *Vernon's Civil Statutes of Texas vol. 9* (Kansas City: Vernon Law Book Co., 1952), xxii.
20 Conrey Bryson, "El Paso and the Poll Tax," *Password 4* (El Paso County Historical Society, 1959), 46.
21 Interview, Dr. L. A. Nixon, El Paso, Texas, July 1944.

22 *General Laws of Texas 38th Legislature,* 2d called sess. (Austin: 1923).
23 Charles C. Alexander, *The Ku Klux Klan in the Southwest* (Lexington: University of Kentucky Press, 1965), 123.
24 *Congressional Record,* 68th Cong., 2d sess. (1925), 2929-30.
25 Alexander, 127.
26 *House Journal,* 38th Legislature, 2d called sess. (Austin: 1923), April 25, 295.
27 *El Paso Times,* April 26, 1923.
28 *El Paso Times,* April 27, 1923.
29 *Senate Journal,* 38th Legislature, and called sess. (Austin: 1923), May 1, 112.
30 Seth S. McKay and Odie B. Faulk, *Texas After Spindletop* (Austin: Steck-Vaughn Co., 1965), 85.
31 *Senate Journal,* 38th Legislature, 2d called sess. (Austin: 1923), 163, 177, 231, 232.
32 Ibid., 305, 342, 376.
33 Ibid., 378, 458.
34 *General Laws of Texas,* 38th Legislature, 2d called sess. (Austin: 1923), 74.
35 Ibid.
36 Interview, Mrs. L. A. Nixon, El Paso, Texas, March 1973.
37 L. A. Nixon Papers, Document 1, Box 1 (Austin, Lyndon Baines Johnson Library); hereafter cited as Nixon Papers.
38 Interview, Dr. L. A. Nixon, El Paso, Texas, July 1944, and Mrs. L. A. Nixon, El Paso, Texas, March 1973.
39 Alexander, 66-67.
40 Kenneth T. Jackson, *The Klux Klan in the City* (New York: Oxford University Press, 1967), 83.
41 Jackson, 71.
42 Jackson, 22.
43 Jackson, 75-76; Alexander, 96.
44 John Middagh, *Frontier Newspaper, The El Paso Times* (El Paso: Texas Western Press, 1958), 201-03.
45 Middagh, 209.
46 Robert Ewing Thomason, *Thomason, the Autobiography of a Federal Judge,* ed. Joseph M. Ray (El Paso: Texas Western Press, 1971), 16.
47 Richard M. Dudley Scrapbook (Archives, El Paso Public Library).
48 Middagh, 213.
49 Richard F. Dudley Scrapbooks, folder 573.
50 "Proceedings of American Federation of Labor Annual Convention, 1923," Friday morning session, October 12, 1923 (in Richard M. Dudley Scrapbooks).

51 El Paso *Times*, October 23, 1923.

52 McKay and Faulk, 89-91.

53 Harry Hanson, ed., *Texas, a Guide to the Lone Star State* (New York: Hastings House, 1969), 200, 534.

54 *Marshall Tri-Weekly Herald*, November 4, 6, 9, 1886.

55 Ira G. Clark, *Then Came the Railroads* (Norman: University of Oklahoma Press, 1968), 68.

56 Texas Highway Department, *Texas, Land of Contrasts* (Austin: Texas Highway Department, 1972), 87.

57 Mrs. L. A. Nixon, El Paso, Texas, August 31, 1973.

58 Ibid.

59 Letter, Mrs. Nixon, September 22, 1973.

60 Rice, 100-111; Walter Prescott Webb, ed., *Texas Handbook* (Austin: Texas Historical Association, 1952), v 2: 485.

61 Nixon to White, February 25, 1952 (Mrs. L. A. Nixon, El Paso).

62 Letter, Mrs. Nixon, September 22, 1973.

63 Max Russell, ed. dir., *The College Blue Book* (New York: C. C. M. Info. Corp., 1969), 203.

64 Letter, Mrs. Nixon, September 22, 1973.

65 Ibid.

66 Mrs. Nixon, March 1973.

67 Tuskegee Institute, *Negro Yearbook* (Tuskegee, Alabama, 1952), 132.

68 El Paso *Times*, December 19, 1909.

69 National Association for the Advancement of Colored People, *The American Negro, His History and Literature*, vol. 110, *Thirty Years of Lynching in the United States* (New York: Arno Press and New York Times, 1969), 21.

70 *El Paso Times*, December 2, 1909.

71 Winfield H. Collins, *The Truth about Lynching and the Negro in the South* (New York: Neale Publishing Co., 1918), 58, 59.

72 *El Paso Times*, December 19, 1909.

73 Letter, Mrs. Nixon, September 22, 1973.

74 *El Paso Times*, December 2, 1909.

75 Interviews, Mrs. L. A. Nixon, March, 1973; Mrs. B. F. Stevens, El Paso, Texas, October 1973.

76 Pat Ireland Nixon, M. D., *A History of the Texas Medical Association, 1853-1953* (Austin: University of Texas Press, 1953), 431.

77 Mrs. Nixon, August 1973.

78 Nixon Papers, box 2, documents 191-197.

79 Interview, Mrs. Robert Roy, daughter of Fred C. Knollenberg, El Paso, Texas, December 1, 1973.

80 Nixon Papers, box 2, document 194.

81 Mrs. Robert Roy, December 1, 1973.
82 Ibid.
83 "Reply to State of Texas Brief," Nixon Papers, box 2, document 229.
84 "Copy of Exhibit A." Nixon Papers, box 2, document 198.
85 Nixon Papers, box 1, document 2.
86 *Nixon v. Herndon and Porras,* 994 Law, U.S. District Court, Western District of Texas.
87 Ibid.
88 Ibid., Defendant's Motion to Dismiss.
89 Ibid., Defendant's Brief.
90 U.S. Statutes, Sec. 1979 and 2004, quoted in "Plaintiff's Brief," *Nixon v. Herndon,* 994 Law.
91 *Nixon v. Herndon,* "Judges Decision," 994 Law.
92 Ibid., Assignment of Errors.
93 Ibid., Writ of Error.
94 White to Knollenberg, September 10, 1925, Nixon Papers, box 1, document 25.
95 Nixon Papers, box 1, document 2.
96 Nixon Papers, box 1, documents 43, 82, 83.
97 Nixon Papers, box 1, documents 31, 33.
98 Nixon Papers, box 1, documents 38, 39.
99 Nixon Papers, box 1, 60, 66, 78.
100 Nixon Papers, box 1, documents 51, 55.
101 Nixon Papers, box 1, document 86.
102 Nixon Papers, box 1, documents 76, 82.
103 *Nixon v. Herndon,* 273 U.S. 536, 760.
104 Nixon Papers, box 1, documents, 91, 92.
105 *Nixon v. Herndon,* 273 U.S. 760.
106 *Nixon v. Herndon,* 273 U.S. 541-2.
107 Nixon Papers, box 1, documents 98, 102.
108 Ralph W. Steen, *Twentieth Century Texas* (Austin: Steck Co., 1942), 302; Dallas Morning News, Texas Almanac, 1972-73, 530.
109 Nixon Papers, box 1, document 90.
110 *House Journal,* 40th Legislature, 1st called sess. (Austin: 1927), 207.
111 Ibid., 246.
112 Ibid., 302.
113 General and Special Laws of Texas, 40th Legislature (Austin: 1927), 207.
114 *Nixon v. Herndon,* 994 Law, U.S. District Court, Western District of Texas.
115 *Nixon v. Condon and Kolle,* 1379 Law, U.S. District Court of Texas.
116 Nixon Papers, box 2, document 330.

117 Nixon Papers, box 2, documents 334, 361.
118 Nixon Papers, box 1, documents 112, 114; box 2, document 350.
119 Nixon Papers, box 2, document 389.
120 Nixon Papers, box 2, document 394.
121 Nixon Papers, box 2, documents 407-410.
122 Nixon Papers, box 2, documents 422, 426, 434-36.
123 *Nixon v. Condon*, Plaintiff's Petition, 1379 Law, U.S. District Court, Western District of Texas.
124 Ibid., Defendant's Motion to Dismiss.
125 Ibid., Opinion of Court.
126 Nixon Papers, box 2, document 802.
127 Nixon Papers, box 2, documents 807, 809, 813.
128 Nixon Papers, box 2, documents 612, 616, 655.
129 Nixon Papers, box 2, document 679.
130 *Nixon v. Condon*, 46 Federal (2d) 1012.
131 Nixon Papers, box 2, documents 523-561.
132 Nixon Papers, box 1, document 178.
133 *Nixon v. Condon*, 286 U.S. 81-89.
134 *Nixon v. Condon*, 1379 Law, U.S. District Court, Western District of Texas, Judgment of the Court.
135 *Nixon v. Condon*, 286 U.S. 84-85.
136 Original letters, Mrs. L. A. Nixon, El Paso, Texas.
137 Nixon Papers, box 1, documents 187, 188, 189.
138 *West v. Bailey*, 33 Fed. (2d) 177.
139 Nixon Papers, box 1, documents 169, 170, 174, 175.
140 *Grovey v. Townsend*, 295 U.S. 45-79.
141 Samuel Eliot Morison, *The Oxford History of the American People* (New York: Oxford University Press, 1965), 969-70.
142 *Smith v. Allwright*, 131 Fed. (2d) 593.
143 *Congressional Directory*, 92d Congress, 1st sess. (Washington: U.S. Government Printing Office, 1971), 683.
144 *Who's Who in America*, 1972-73, 360.
145 *Smith v. Allwright*, 321 U.S. 649-70.
146 Ibid., 663, 664.
147 *El Paso Herald-Post*, July 19, 1944.
148 *El Paso Times*, July 20, 1944.
149 *El Paso Times*, July 23, 1944; *El Paso Herald-Post*, July 22, 1944.
150 Nixon to White, February 25, 1952. (Mrs. L. A. Nixon, El Paso, Texas.)
151 Nixon Papers, box 1, document 167.
152 Nixon Papers, box 2, document 394.
153 Interview, Mrs. L. A. Nixon, El Paso, Texas, February, 1974.

154 Lyndon Baines Johnson, *The Vantage Point* (New York: Rinehart, Holt and Winston, 1971), 161.
155 Minutes, El Paso Independent School District, June 21, 1955.
156 *Thelma White v. A. A. Smith, Texas Western College,* 1616 Law, U.S. District Court, Western District of Texas, 1955.
157 *El Paso City Code,* Ordinance 2698, June 21, 1962 (City of El Paso, Texas), sec. 15-2-1.
158 *El Paso City Code,* Ordinance 4324, December 18, 1969 (City of El Paso, Texas), sec. 7A-13.
159 Interviews, Mr. and Mrs. Fred Ward, El Paso, Texas, February 1974.
160 *Texas State Journal of Medicine,* June 1955, 379-81.
161 Nixon Way runs eastward from Douglass School, south of Tays Housing Project.
162 Copy, Mrs. L. A. Nixon, El Paso, Texas.
163 Nixon to White, February 25, 1952, Mrs. L. A. Nixon, El Paso, Texas.

ABOUT THE AUTHOR

Conrey Bryson, born in Utah, has lived in El Paso since 1929. He holds BA and MA degrees in history from the University of Texas at El Paso, has taught there and at El Paso Community College, and is a member of the UTEP Heritage Commission. His interest in Doctor Nixon and negro suffrage came during his twenty-eight-year career in news and special events for KTSM Radio and Television. He became acquainted with Dr. and Mrs. Nixon and featured the Nixon story in various programs. Mr. Bryson served for twelve years as a member of the El Paso Public Service Board. His master's thesis, "El Paso Water Supply," reflects this service. In 1965, he was chosen by Congressman Richard C. White to be his administrative assistant in Washington, where he served until his retirement in 1972. Since his retirement he has been active in church work for the Church of Jesus Christ of Latter-day Saints, civic affairs, writing, and travel. He served three terms as president of the El Paso County Historical Society and for five years as editor of its quarterly, *Password*. He was selected in 1973 to write *The Land Where We Live,* a centennial history of El Paso, for Aniversario del Paso. His book, *Down Went McGinty,* published by Texas Western Press in 1977, was the first winner of the Sonnichsen Award for the best book on El Paso history and culture. In 1986, Deseret Book Company of Salt Lake City published his book, *Winter Quarters,* an account of the vital way-station in Nebraska for the Mormon migration to Utah in 1846-47. His first wife, Pat, who died in 1972, was for many years librarian of the Memorial Branch, El Paso Public Library. In 1974, he married Mrs. Fay Gardner Maxwell, who died in 1992.